Trent P. Kynaston is a professor of music
at Western Michigan University in Kalamazoo, Michigan.

Robert J. Ricci is a professor of music
and chairman of the theory area
at Western Michigan University
in Kalamazoo, Michigan.

Jazz improvisation

TRENT P. KYNASTON
ROBERT J. RICCI

A SPECTRUM BOOK

Prentice-Hall, Inc., Englewood Cliffs, N.J. 07632

Library of Congress Cataloging in Publication Data

KYNASTON, TRENT P
  Jazz improvisation.

  (A Spectrum Book)
  Includes index.
    1. Improvisation (Music) 2. Jazz music.
I. Ricci, Robert, joint author. II. Title.
MT68.K95   781.6'5   77-28290
ISBN 0-13-509315-5
ISBN 0-13-509307-4 pbk.

©1978 by Prentice-Hall, Inc., *Englewood Cliffs, N.J. 07632*

A SPECTRUM BOOK

Printed in the United States of America

10 9 8 7 6 5 4 3 2 1

PRENTICE-HALL INTERNATIONAL, INC., *London*
PRENTICE-HALL OF AUSTRALIA PTY. LIMITED, *Sydney*
PRENTICE-HALL OF CANADA, LTD., *Toronto*
PRENTICE-HALL OF INDIA PRIVATE LIMITED, *New Delhi*
PRENTICE-HALL OF JAPAN, INC., *Tokyo*
PRENTICE-HALL OF SOUTHEAST ASIA PTE. LTD., *Singapore*
WHITEHALL BOOKS LIMITED, *Wellington, New Zealand*

Contents

The study
of jazz
improvisation

Chapter 1

(2) Jazz is a highly involved American art form that has become a major influence on all types of music, dance, and related arts throughout the world. A brief look at its history shows that it evolved as a blending of the musical cultures of Africa and Europe during the first three hundred years of American development. In examining the elements of early jazz, we find that the scales, the melodic forms, most of the instruments, and indeed even the rhymed couplet of early blues lyrics (iambic pentameter) are primarily of classical European origins. Yet the influence of African traditions is by far the most important element, for without these traditions the true essence of jazz would not exist. The importance and predominance of rhythm and the idea of individual interpretation are truly African in origin. The role of rhythm in jazz is, at least on the surface, somewhat obvious and needs no special attention at this time. However, the element of interpretation—that is, the concept that jazz is a performer's art and not a composer's art—deserves further discussion.

The idea of interpretation allows the player of jazz to perform the music the way his/her consciousness and soul interpret it and not necessarily the way the composer, if any, specifically intended it. Jazz performers may choose the tempo, dynamics, and the rhythm they feel best fits their own understanding of the music, and also decide how much to ornament the original melody. This may result in an easily recognizable tune or one so altered that its original form is not recognizable. This process is the true essence of jazz, from which the art of jazz improvisation has evolved. This is not to say that the idea of improvisation in itself is a product of jazz. Improvisation can be found in every musical style and culture, but in jazz it is the predominant and driving force.

A number of skills related to basic musicianship are needed before beginning this text. These are covered in most public school music programs, and we discuss them here only to highlight their importance. The ability to read music is of prime importance. This seems to represent somewhat of a paradox, because improvisation in its essence requires no reading, either of notes or of chord changes. It only requires that you hear and be able to transfer what you hear to your instrument. But in today's world, your musical existence is related to your ability to read music, and you would be wise to develop this skill to its fullest extent.

You should also master basic technical facilities before beginning a study of improvisation. All major and minor keys must be memorized and scales mastered before chords and jazz scales can be fully utilized and understood. The finger technique developed from this is extremely important and will prove valuable in the studies to follow. Basic skills in ear training are also necessary. This is somewhat of an understatement, because the degree of proficiency you reach in developing your ear will be the single most crucial factor in developing the skill of improvising. At the beginning, it is highly advisable for you to learn to recognize simple intonations and pitch relationships or intervals, and your ability to write these out and explore their sounds at the piano will be extremely helpful.

Along with these skills there are others, just as basic, that need special attention. No matter how advanced you are as a "classical" performer, you should approach jazz improvisation at the ground level, with the same dedication given more advanced study. When the jazz musician tells you, the novice, "You have to learn your axe," he means that you have to learn to transfer musical thoughts you have in your head into tonal reality on your instrument. This means primarily training your ear, as well as learning the sound and feel of all the notes on your instrument. For instance, can you put on a record, listen to the first phrase, and then go to your instrument and play it, note for note, the first time? If the answer is no, find another student interested in developing these same skills and begin practice on matching tones. One should play a series of single notes while the other attempts to find them on his instrument. When the matching of single notes becomes easier, proceed to two-note phrases and subsequently to three-, four-, and five-note phrases. Transfer this idea of matching phrases to things heard on the radio and recordings, and if you really like what you hear, write it down for further study.

Along with developing your ear in relation to your instrument, you must also constantly search for an individual sound concept. In "classical" music, there is a more or less traditional sound that everyone playing your instrument is supposed to obtain. In jazz, no one told Stanley Turrentine that he must sound like Stan Getz, or Urbie Green that he must match J. J. Johnson's sound, or Miles Davis that he should sound like Dizzy Gillespie. Indeed, if they were told anything at all, it was to sound like themselves and not to copy someone else's style or predetermination of what is good or bad. You may spend many years experimenting, changing equipment, and listening to others before you have a complete concept of what *your* sound should be. You must be aware now of the need to search out this identity, because it can have a decided effect on your whole approach to improvisation.

Jazz is never performed exactly the way it is notated. The rhythm, articulation, and phrasing used in jazz evolve from the individual's interpretation of what is placed on the page or heard, and these elements are used much the same way in improvisation. It is all but impossible to teach the intuitive use of these nuances, as they change from instrument to instrument and style to style. Again, the key to acquiring these skills is listening to recordings, imitating stylistic traits, and incorporating them into your own playing. The importance of listening cannot be stressed too highly and will be referred to throughout the text.

Another abstract skill that must be recognized and mastered is a sense of time. Here we refer to rhythm as it relates to phrasing and the passage of time (seconds and minutes, etc.). Many students begin improvising a solo only to stop in frustration because they are lost. They do not know where they are in the structure of the tune. This may be partially caused by the inability to "hear" the chord changes, but it is largely due to inability to conceive the passage of rhythmic time as it is related to the composition being performed. Again, years of total involvement with jazz is the answer.

In your development as a musician, remember that you cannot succeed without total dedication and involvement. In music you win no championship without perfection. Success in improvisation will come only to the student who will not settle for less than perfection and who dedicates himself to the time and work involved in achieving it.

Jazz chords and chord charts

Chapter 2

(6)

Jazz is a seventh-chord idiom. The seventh chord serves as the basis of the jazz harmonic idiom. Chords larger than sevenths are, of course, also common. Chords smaller than seventh chords (triads) are infrequently utilized.

As the basis of seventh chords we have the four types of triads: major, minor, diminished, and augmented. These are shown below in Example 1 with their intervallic structure listed alongside.

EXAMPLE 1

a) Major   b) Minor   c) Augmented   d) Diminished

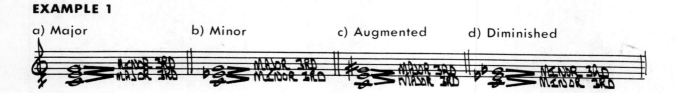

In jazz nomenclature these four triads would be indicated by the following symbols:

a) C
b) Cm
c) C⁺
d) C°

The seventh chords are extensions of these basic triad types. In Example 2, we see the five most common types of seventh chords. Chords (a) and (b) are constructed upon major triads, (c) upon a minor triad, (d) and (e) upon diminished triads. The common chord symbols are indicated below each chord.

EXAMPLE 2

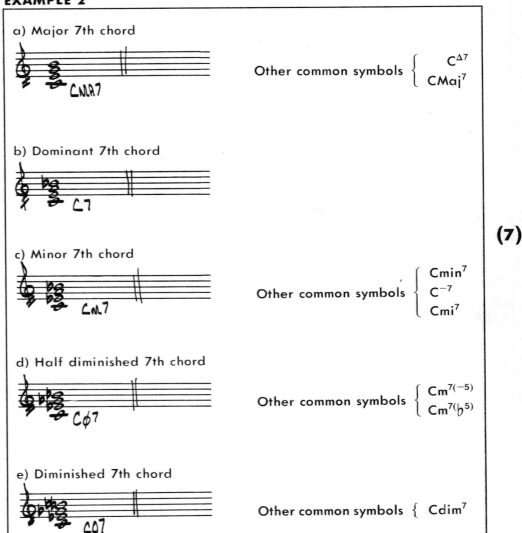

a) Major 7th chord

$C_{MA}7$

Other common symbols $\left\{ \begin{array}{l} C^{\Delta7} \\ CMaj^7 \end{array} \right.$

b) Dominant 7th chord

$C7$

c) Minor 7th chord

$C_{Mi}7$

Other common symbols $\left\{ \begin{array}{l} Cmin^7 \\ C^{-7} \\ Cmi^7 \end{array} \right.$

d) Half diminished 7th chord

$C\phi7$

Other common symbols $\left\{ \begin{array}{l} Cm^{7(-5)} \\ Cm^{7(\flat5)} \end{array} \right.$

e) Diminished 7th chord

$C07$

Other common symbols $\{\ Cdim^7$

Other types of seventh chords are also possible, but are less common. Example 3(a) shows a minor triad with a major seventh on top. 3(b) illustrates a dominant seventh chord with a raised fifth, and 3(c) shows a dominant seventh chord with a lowered fifth. Both 3(b) and 3(c) occur in jazz as modifications of the basic dominant seventh chord.

EXAMPLE 3

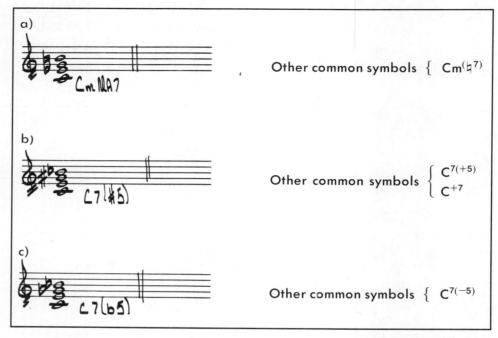

a)

CmMA7

Other common symbols { Cm(♮7)

b)

C7(♯5)

Other common symbols { C7(+5) C+7

c)

C7(♭5)

Other common symbols { C7(−5)

Jazz also utilizes so-called sixth chords. These chords are formed by the addition of an intervallic sixth above a basic triad type. Example 4 shows the two common sixth chords. Note that the sixth in both cases lies a *major* sixth above the root of the chord. Since one of the chords is called major and the other minor, it is a common error to suppose that the sixth is altered to form the minor sixth chord.

EXAMPLE 4

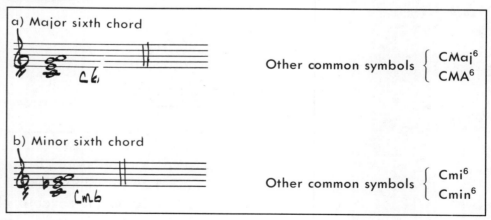

a) Major sixth chord

C6

Other common symbols { CMaj6 CMA6

b) Minor sixth chord

Cm6

Other common symbols { Cmi6 Cmin6

Any seventh chord may be extended by the addition of ninths, elevenths, and thirteenths. For purposes of simplicity the seventh chord types are listed below with the additions *commonly found* indicated alongside. Obviously, any note can be added to any chord. But in jazz, certain additions are common, while others are virtually never found. Note that regardless of the type of seventh chord the basic ninths, elevenths, and thirteenths found as additions stem from the major scale unless altered via a sharp or flat.

EXAMPLE 5

SUSPENDED FOURTH CHORD A chord quite common in much of today's jazz is the so-called "sus. 4" chord. Since the middle 1960s this chord occurs more and more frequently in many different tonal contexts. Sometimes it is used as a substitute for a dominant seventh chord; sometimes it elides into a dominant seventh chord; or, on occasion it has a function all its own, outside the dominant-to-tonic harmonic pattern. The chord is most easily visualized as a dominant seventh chord minus the third, with the "sus. 4" taking its place a perfect fourth above the root of the chord:

EXAMPLE 6

Example 7a illustrates the sus. 4 chord utilized as a dominant replacement moving to tonic major and tonic minor:

EXAMPLE 7

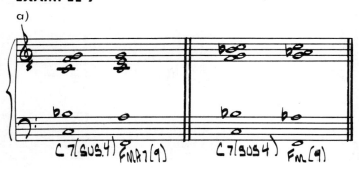

Example 7b illustrates the sus. 4 chord eliding into the "regular" dominant seventh chord, which is then followed by a tonic resolution:

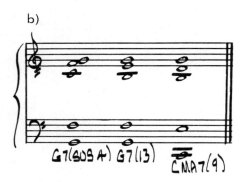

Example 7c illustrates the sus. 4 chord unrelated to dominant-tonic movements, but rather as an independent chord with a sequential life generated by root movements other than by fifths, as in the two earlier examples. This kind of harmonic syntax is similar to tunes such as "Maiden Voyage," "Fancy Free," and "Cantaloupe Island."

c)

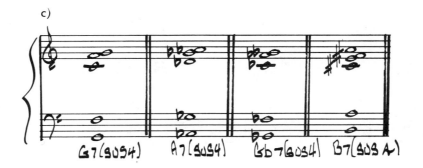

G7(sus4)   A7(sus4)   Gb7(sus4)   B7(sus4)

QUARTAL HARMONY A chord closely related to the sus. 4 structure is the quartal chord, a sonority constructed in perfect fourths. Although quartal harmony could embrace other kinds of fourths as building blocks (e.g., diminished and augmented fourths), it is the perfect fourth that is most often found as the interval upon which these chords are constructed. Quartal harmony as a musical element has been present for most of the twentieth century, but it is only in recent years that it has found its way into jazz. We propose a new system of chord symbols for these structures, since none have been successfully codified as yet. For a basic quartal chord, consisting of three pitches, each a perfect fourth apart, the letter (Q) would be placed next to the chord root. Hence:

(11)

EXAMPLE 8

a)

G(Q)   A(Q)   Bb(Q)   Eb(Q)

When a quartal chord is extended past a three-note structure a small arabic numeral can be utilized next to the (Q) to indicate precisely the number of notes in the chord.

b)

C(Q4)   C(Q5)   Eb(Q6)

The following chart lists chromatically and in sequence thirty-eight of the most commonly encountered jazz chords. The keys are indicated down the left side of each page with the chord types listed across the top. Note that each column of chord types is numbered for later use with the Chord-Function-Scale chart in Chapter IV.

Practice spelling chords of all types in all keys and use this chart to check your accuracy.

BDFACE → CEGBDF

This is a chord chart with twelve root rows (one per chromatic pitch) and ten chord-quality columns.

	1 MA	2 m	3 MA⁶	4 m⁶	5 MA⁷	6 MA⁷⁺⁵	7 MA⁷♭⁵	8 7	9 7(sus 4)	10 m⁷
C										
D♭ (D♭ E♭ G♭ A♭ B♭)										
D (F♯ C♯)										
E♭ (E♭ A♭ B♭)										
E (F♯ G♯ C♯ D♯)										
F (B♭)										
F♯ (F♯ G♯ A♯ C♯ D♯)										
G (F♯)										
A♭ (A♭ B♭ D♭ E♭)										
A (C♯ F♯ G♯)										
B♭ (B♭ E♭)										
B (C♯ D♯ F♯ G♯ A♯)										

(12)

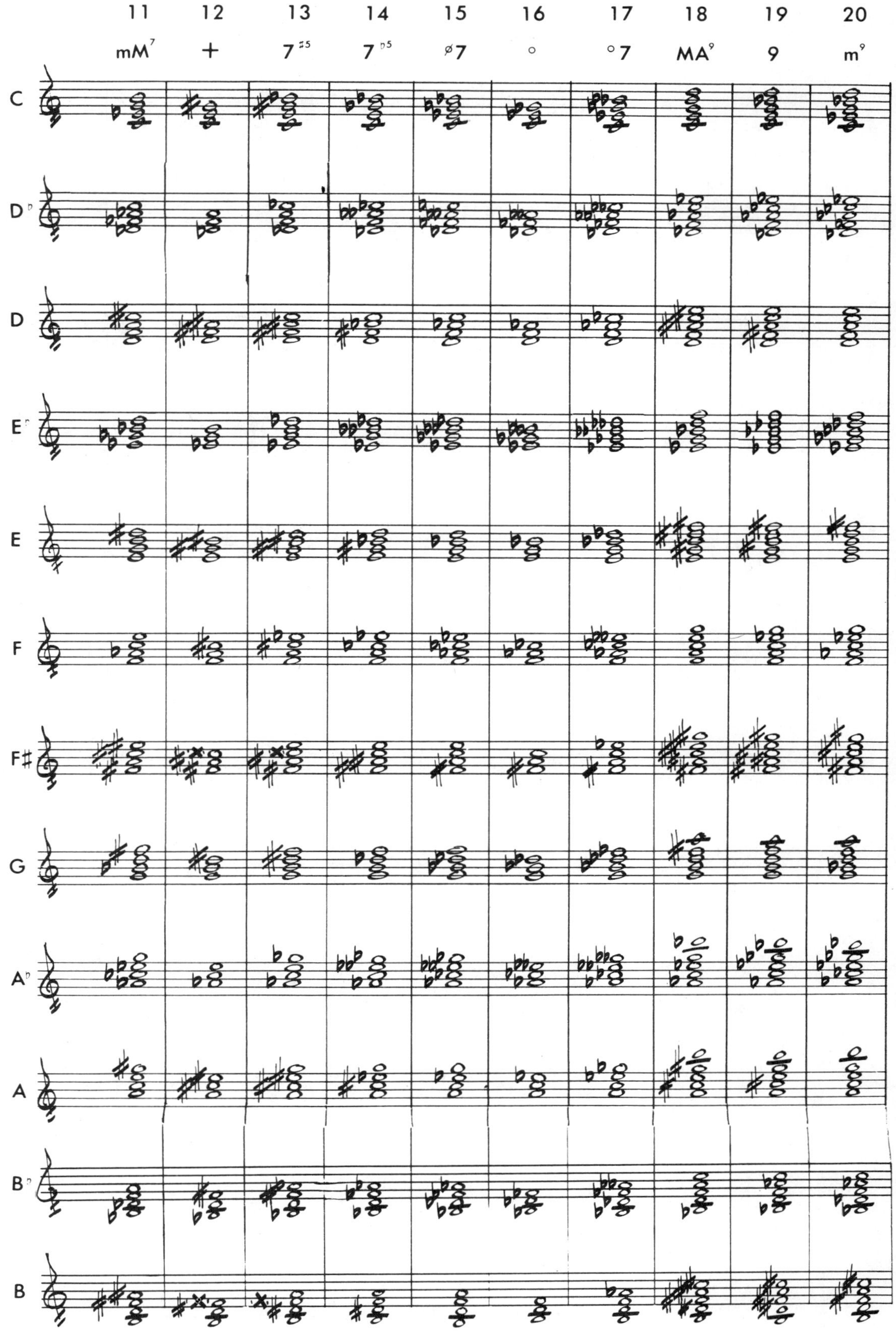
11 12 13 14 15 16 17 18 19 20
mM7 + 7♯5 7♭5 ø7 ° °7 MA9 9 m9
C
D♭
D
E♭
E
F
F♯
G
A♭
A
B♭
B

BDFACE CEGBDF

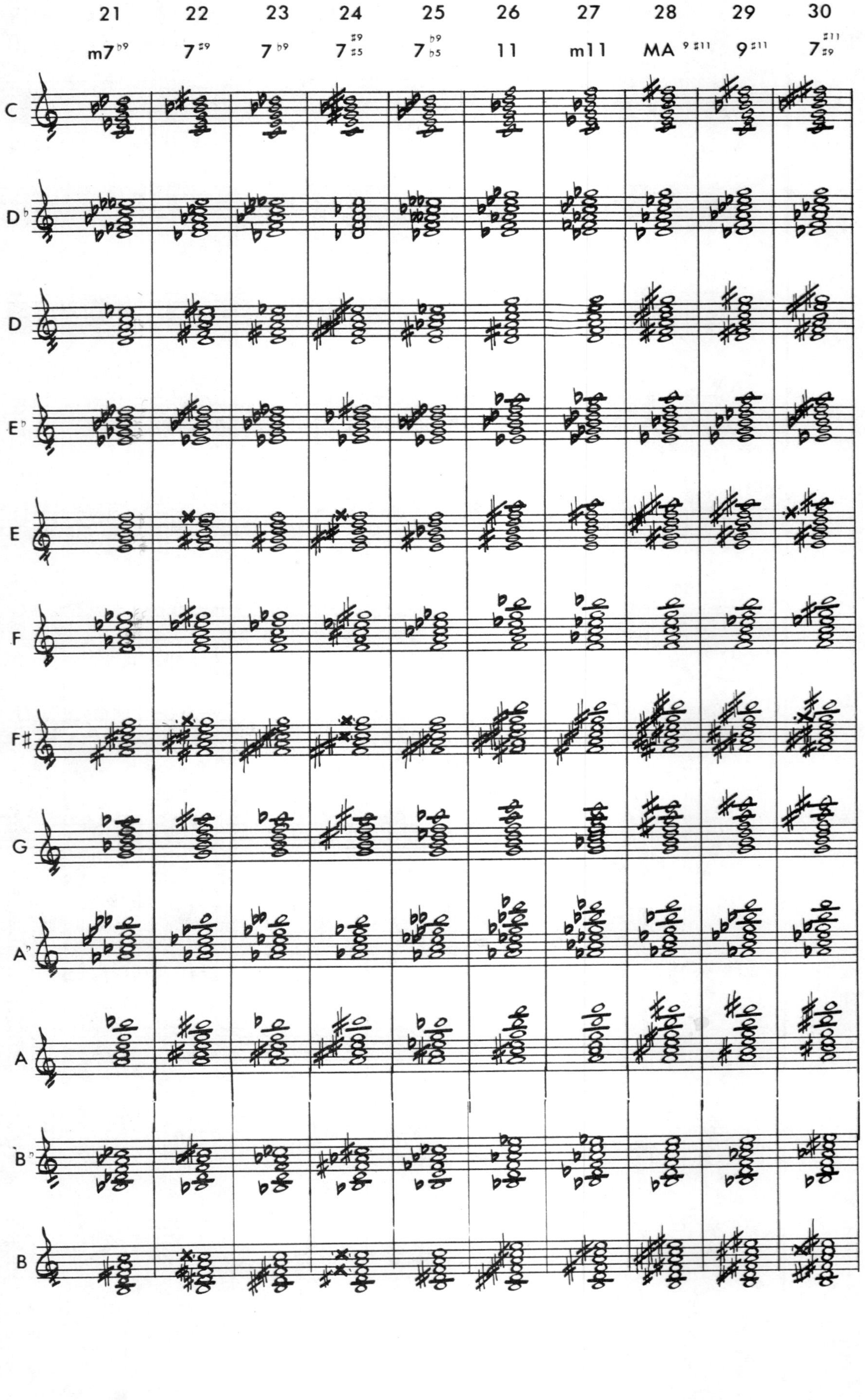

(14)

(15)

Jazz scales and scale chart

Chapter 3

Jazz makes use of all common major, minor, and modal scales, along with many others that are unique and colorful. The following chart presents these scales, their patterns, and an example of each. This is followed by the complete chromatic setting of each scale. Note that there are 19 scale patterns to learn and 12 chromatic settings of each, for a total of 128 scales.

This chart will also serve as reference material when you are working with the Chord–Function–Scale chart in Chapter IV. Learn the pattern and note the relative sound of each scale presented.

Jazz Scale Forms   ($\vee$ = 1/2 step: $\sqcup$ = 1 1/2 steps)

Scale	Pattern	Example
Major	1 2 3 $\vee$ 4 5 6 7 $\vee$ 8	C Major 
Dorian	1 2 $\flat$3 4 5 6 $\flat$7 8	C Dorian 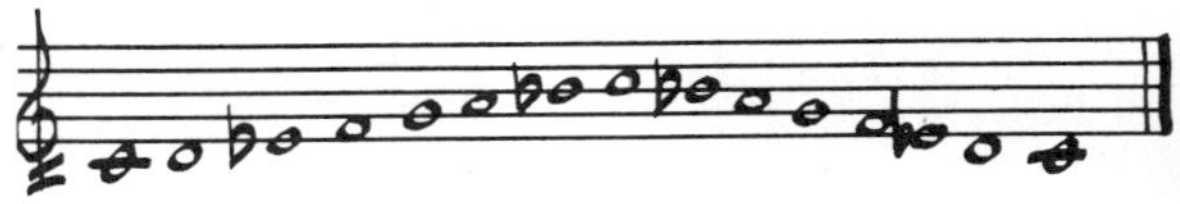

Jazz Scale Forms (continued)

Scale	Pattern	Example
Phrygian	1 ♭2 ♭3 4 5 ♭6 ♭7 8	C Phrygian 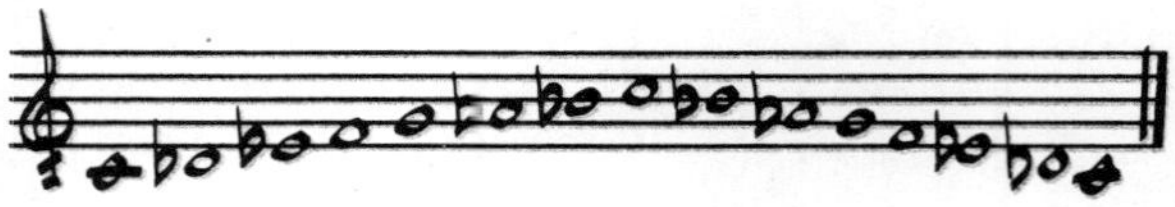
Lydian	1 2 3 ♯4 5 6 7 8	C Lydian 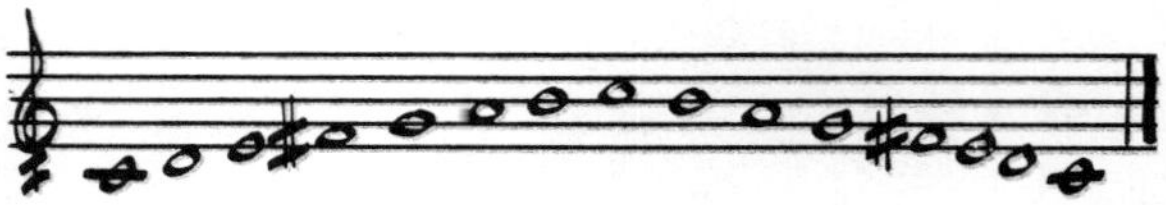
Mixolydian	1 2 3 4 5 6 ♭7 8	C Mixolydian 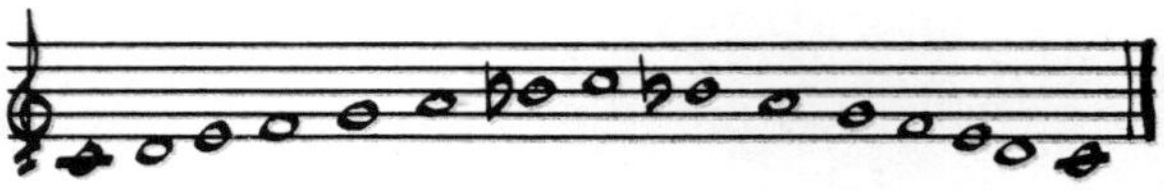
Aeolian	1 2 ♭3 4 5 ♭6 ♭7 8	C Aeolian 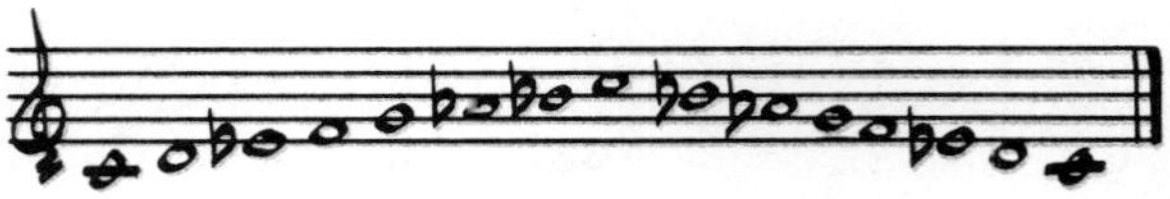
Locrian	1 ♭2 ♭3 4 ♭5 ♭6 ♭7 8	C Locrian 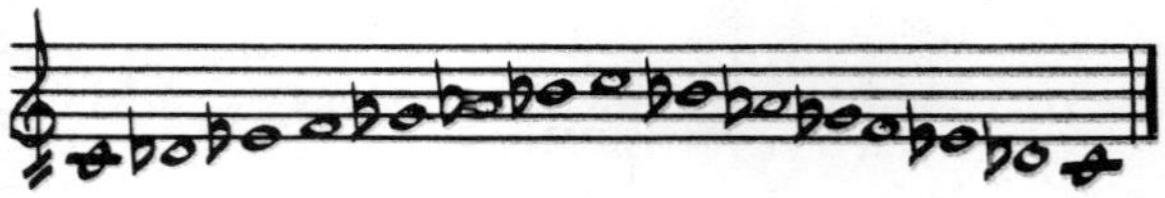
Melodic Minor (Jazz Form)	1 2 ♭3 4 5 6 7 8	C Melodic Minor (same ascending and descending) 
Harmonic Minor	1 2 ♭3 4 5 ♭6 7 8	C Harmonic Minor 
Whole-Tone	1 2 3 ♯4 ♯5 ♭7 8	C Whole-Tone 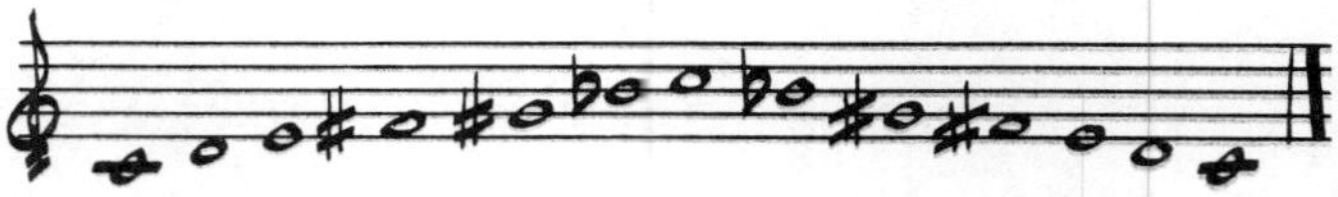

(18)

Jazz Scale Forms (continued)

Scale	Pattern	Example
Diminished	1 2 ♭3 4 ♯4 ♯5 6 7 8	C Diminished
Blues	1 ♭3 3 4 ♯4 5 ♭7 8	C Blues
Pentatonic	1 2 4 5 6 8	C Pentatonic

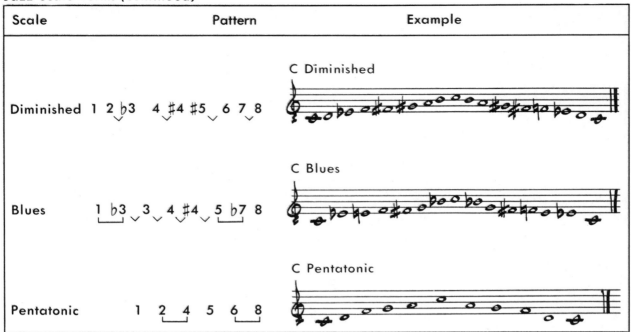

NOTE: The auxiliary diminished, lydian/mixolydian (lydian—flat seven), and lydian augmented scales are presented in many improvisation methods as functional scales, distinct and different from any other. As you will note in the example below, the notes in these scales can be obtained by using corresponding scales that are much more common. Rather than suggest that a student learn these additional scales in all their chromatic settings, the authors will not refer to the auxiliary diminished but rather to its corresponding diminished scale, not to the lydian/mixolydian but to its corresponding melodic minor scale, and not to the lydian augmented but to its corresponding melodic minor scale.

EXAMPLE 1

B Auxiliary Diminished = C Diminished

F Lydian/Mixolydian = C Melodic Minor

E♭ Lydian Augmented = C Melodic Minor

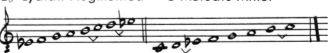

Auxiliary and Exotic Scale Forms

Scale	Pattern	Example

Auxiliary Blues (1)

1 2 ♭3 3 4 5 6 ♭7 8

C Auxiliary Blues (1)

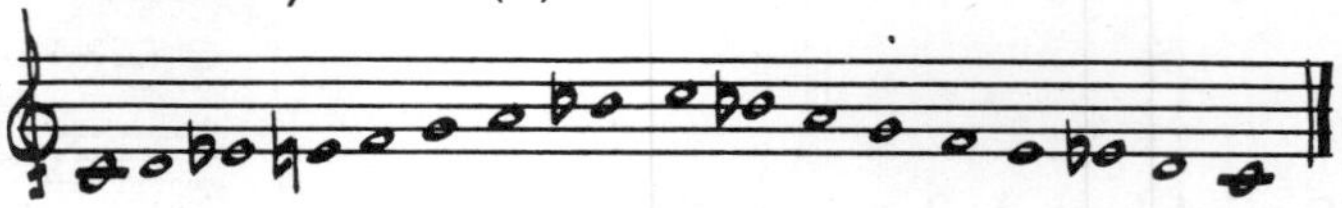

Auxiliary Blues (2)

1 2 ♭3 3 4 ♯4 5 6 ♭7 8

C Auxiliary Blues (2)

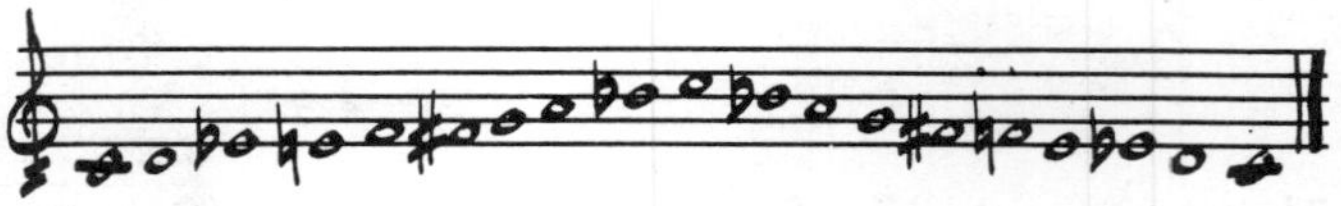

Gypsy Minor

1 ♭2 3 4 5 ♭6 7 8

C Gypsy Minor

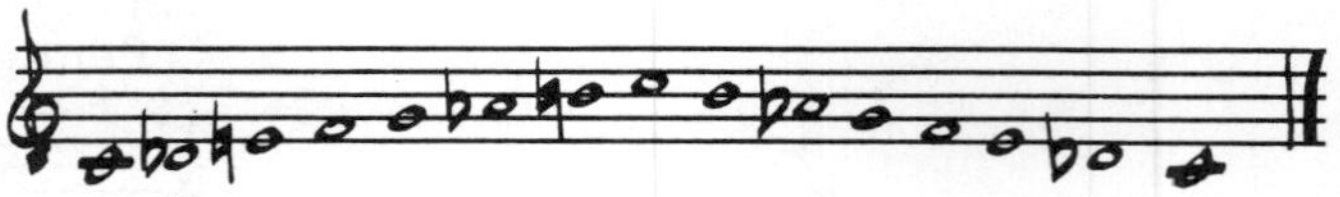

(20)

Augmented Gypsy Minor

1 2 ♭3 ♯4 5 ♭6 7 8

C Augmented Gypsy Minor

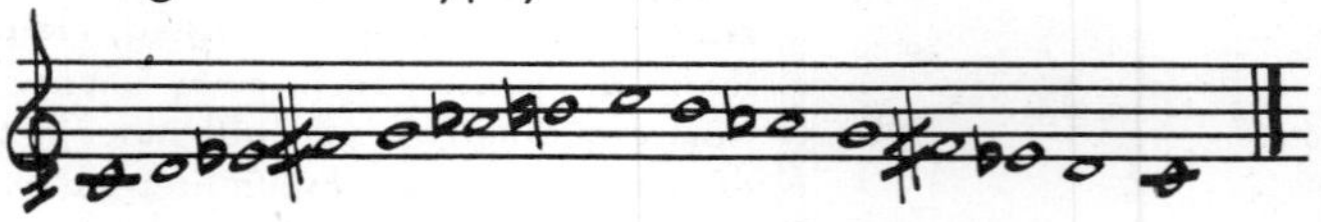

Composite (1)

1 ♭2 ♭3 3 ♯4 5 ♭6 ♭7 8

C Composite (1)

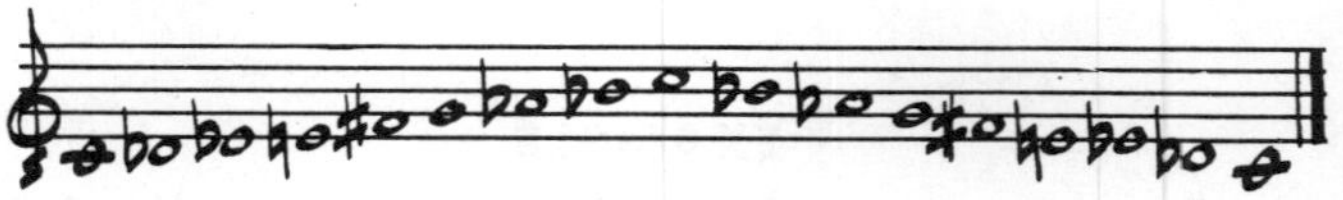

Composite (2)

1 2 ♭3 4 ♯4 ♯5 6 ♭7 8

C Composite (2)

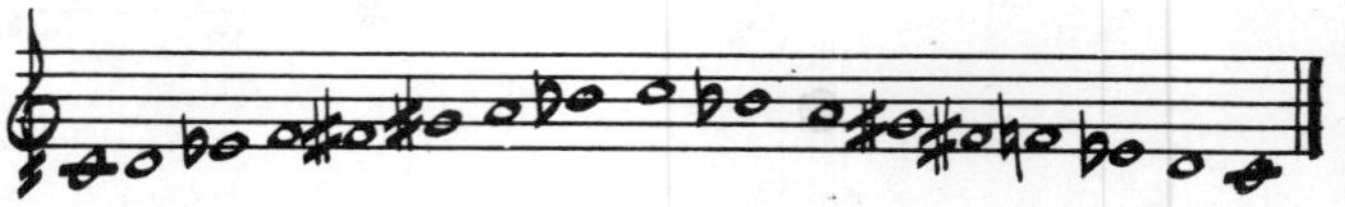

Major Scale

C	D	E	F	G	A	B	C
F	G	A	Bb	C	D	E	F
Bb	C	D	Eb	F	G	A	Bb
Eb	F	G	Ab	Bb	C	D	Eb
Ab	Bb	C	Db	Eb	F	G	Ab
Db	Eb	F	Gb	Ab	Bb	C	Db
F#	G#	A#	B	C#	D#	E#	F#
B	C#	D#	E	F#	G#	A#	B
E	F#	G#	A	B	C#	D#	E
A	B	C#	D	E	F#	G#	A
D	E	F#	G	A	B	C#	D
G	A	B	C	D	E	F#	G

Dorian Scale

C	D	Eb	F	G	A	Bb	C
F	G	Ab	Bb	C	D	Eb	F
Bb	C	Db	Eb	F	G	Ab	Bb
Eb	F	Gb	Ab	Bb	C	Db	Eb
Ab	Bb	Cb	Db	Eb	F	Gb	Ab
Db	Eb	Fb	Gb	Ab	Bb	Cb	Db
F#	G#	A	B	C#	D#	E	F#
B	C#	D	E	F#	G#	A	B
E	F#	G	A	B	C#	D	E
A	B	C	D	E	F#	G	A
D	E	F	G	A	B	C	D
G	A	Bb	C	D	E	F	G

Phrygian Scale

C	Db	Eb	F	G	Ab	Bb	C
F	Gb	Ab	Bb	C	Db	Eb	F
Bb	Cb	Db	Eb	F	Gb	Ab	Bb
Eb	Fb	Gb	Ab	Bb	Cb	Db	Eb
G#	A	B	C#	D#	E	F#	G#
C#	D	E	F#	G#	A	B	C#
F#	G	A	B	C#	D	E	F#
B	C	D	E	F#	G	A	B
E	F	G	A	B	C	D	E
A	Bb	C	D	E	F	G	A
D	Eb	F	G	A	Bb	C	D
G	Ab	Bb	C	D	Eb	F	G

Lydian Scale

C	D	E	F#	G	A	B	C
F	G	A	B	C	D	E	F
Bb	C	D	E	F	G	A	Bb
Eb	F	G	A	Bb	C	D	Eb
Ab	Bb	C	D	Eb	F	G	Ab
Db	Eb	F	G	Ab	Bb	C	Db
F#	G#	A#	B#	C#	D#	E#	F#
B	C#	D#	E#	F#	G#	A#	B
E	F#	G#	A#	B	C#	D#	E
A	B	C#	D#	E	F#	G#	A
D	E	F#	G#	A	B	C#	D
G	A	B	C#	D	E	F#	G

(21)

Mixolydian Scale

C	D	E	F	G	A	Bb	C
F	G	A	Bb	C	D	Eb	F
Bb	C	D	Eb	F	G	Ab	Bb
Eb	F	G	Ab	Bb	C	Db	Eb
Ab	Bb	C	Db	Eb	F	Gb	Ab
Db	Eb	F	Gb	Ab	Bb	Cb	Db
F#	G#	A#	B	C#	D#	E	F#
B	C#	D#	E	F#	G#	A	B
E	F#	G#	A	B	C#	D	E
A	B	C#	D	E	F#	G	A
D	E	F#	G	A	B	C	D
G	A	B	C	D	E	F	G

Aeolian Scale

C	D	Eb	F	G	Ab	Bb	C
F	G	Ab	Bb	C	Db	Eb	F
Bb	C	Db	Eb	F	Gb	Ab	Bb
Eb	F	Gb	Ab	Bb	Cb	Db	Eb
Ab	Bb	Cb	Db	Eb	Fb	Gb	Ab
C#	D#	E	F#	G#	A	B	C#
F#	G#	A	B	C#	D	E	F#
B	C#	D	E	F#	G	A	B
E	F#	G	A	B	C	D	E
A	B	C	D	E	F	G	A
D	E	F	G	A	Bb	C	D
G	A	Bb	C	D	Eb	F	G

Locrian Scale

C	Db	Eb	F	Gb	Ab	Bb	C
F	Gb	Ab	Bb	Cb	Db	Eb	F
Bb	Cb	Db	Eb	Fb	Gb	Ab	Bb
D#	E	F#	G#	A	B	C#	D#
G#	A	B	C#	D	E	F#	G#
C#	D	E	F#	G	A	B	C#
F#	G	A	B	C	D	E	F#
B	C	D	E	F	G	A	B
E	F	G	A	Bb	C	D	E
A	Bb	C	D	Eb	F	G	A
D	Eb	F	G	Ab	Bb	C	D
G	Ab	Bb	C	Db	Eb	F	G

Jazz Melodic Minor

C	D	Eb	F	G	A	B	C
F	G	Ab	Bb	C	D	E	F
Bb	C	Db	Eb	F	G	A	Bb
Eb	F	Gb	Ab	Bb	C	D	Eb
Ab	Bb	Cb	Db	Eb	F	G	Ab
C#	D#	E	F#	G#	A#	B#	C#
F#	G#	A	B	C#	D#	E#	F#
B	C#	D	E	F#	G#	A#	B
E	F#	G	A	B	C#	D#	E
A	B	C	D	E	F#	G#	A
D	E	F	G	A	B	C#	D
G	A	Bb	C	D	E	F#	G

Harmonic Minor

Whole-Tone

C	D	Eb	F	G	Ab	B	C
F	G	Ab	Bb	C	Db	E	F
Bb	C	Db	Eb	F	Gb	A	Bb
Eb	F	Gb	Ab	Bb	Cb	D	Eb
Ab	Bb	Cb	Db	Eb	Fb	G	Ab
C#	D#	E	F#	G#	A	B#	C#
F#	G#	A	B	C#	D	E#	F#
B	C#	D	E	F#	G	A#	B
E	F#	G	A	B	C	D#	E
A	B	C	D	E	F	G#	A
D	E	F	G	A	Bb	C#	D
G	A	Bb	C	D	Eb	F#	G

C	D	E	F#	G#	Bb	C
F	G	A	B	C#	Eb	F
Bb	C	D	E	F#	Ab	Bb
Eb	F	G	A	B	C#	Eb
Ab	Bb	C	D	E	F#	Ab
Db	Eb	F	G	A	B	Db
Gb	Ab	Bb	C	D	E	Gb
B	C#	Eb	F	G	A	B
E	F#	G#	Bb	C	D	E
A	B	C#	Eb	F	G	A
D	E	F#	G#	Bb	C	D
G	A	B	C#	Eb	F	G

NOTE: That there are, in actuality, only two whole-tone scales.

(23)

Diminished Scale

Pentatonic

C	D	Eb	F	F#	G#	A	B	C
F	G	Ab	Bb	B	C#	D	E	F
Bb	C	Db	Eb	E	F#	G	A	Bb
Eb	F	Gb	Ab	A	B	C	D	Eb
Ab	Bb	Cb	Db	D	E	F	G	Ab
Db	Eb	Fb	Gb	G	A	Bb	C	Db
F#	G#	A	B	C	D	Eb	F	F#
B	C#	D	E	F	G	Ab	Bb	B
E	F#	G	A	Bb	C	Db	Eb	E
A	B	C	D	Eb	F	F#	G#	A
D	E	F	G	Ab	Bb	B	C#	D
G	A	Bb	C	C#	D#	E	F#	G

C	D	F	G	A	C
F	G	Bb	C	D	F
Bb	C	Eb	F	G	Bb
Eb	F	Ab	Bb	C	Eb
Ab	Bb	Db	Eb	F	Ab
Db	Eb	Gb	Ab	Bb	Db
F#	G#	B	C#	D#	F#
B	C#	E	F#	G#	B
E	F#	A	B	C#	E
A	B	D	E	F#	A
D	E	G	A	B	D
G	A	C	D	E	G

How Did Becket -1912 ect. -Never mind- pass on Notes taken jazz & songs
was emerging w/o ~~Notes~~ a scale & clef system - answer 1-ear 2- they
had cleff system ~~even in~~ beginning in motzar's time (period pre 1600?) - when did cleff
system arrive?

Take a
flight of
fancy over
all geographic
terrain w/
the eagle!
inside.

Invention of the saxaphone?

Blues Scale

C	Eb	E	F	F#	G	Bb	C
F	Ab	A	Bb	B	C	Eb	F
Bb	Db	D	Eb	E	F	Ab	Bb
Eb	Gb	G	Ab	A	Bb	Db	Eb
Ab	Cb	C	Db	D	Eb	Gb	Ab
C#	E	E#	F#	G	G#	B	C#
F#	A	A#	B	B#	C#	E	F#
B	D	D#	E	E#	F#	A	B
E	G	G#	A	A#	B	D	E
A	C	C#	D	D#	E	G	A
D	F	F#	G	G#	A	C	D
G	Bb	B	C	C#	D	F	G

| 1 | 2♯ | 3 | 4 | 4♯ | 5 | 7 | 8 |

Auxiliary Blues Scale (1)

C	D	Eb	E	F	G	A	Bb	C
F	G	Ab	A	Bb	C	D	Eb	F
Bb	C	Db	D	Eb	F	G	Ab	Bb
Eb	F	Gb	G	Ab	Bb	C	Db	Eb
Ab	Bb	Cb	C	Db	Eb	F	Gb	Ab
Db	Eb	Fb	F	Gb	Ab	Bb	Cb	Db
F#	G#	A	A#	B	C#	D#	E	F#
B	C#	D	D#	E	F#	G#	A	B
E	F#	G	G#	A	B	C#	D	E
A	B	C	C#	D	E	F#	G	A
D	E	F	F#	G	A	B	C	D
G	A	Bb	B	C	D	E	F	G

(24)

Auxiliary Blues Scale (2)

C	D	Eb	E	F	F#	G	A	Bb	C
F	G	Ab	A	Bb	B	C	D	Eb	F
Bb	C	Db	D	Eb	E	F	G	Ab	Bb
Eb	F	Gb	G	Ab	A	Bb	C	Db	Eb
Ab	Bb	Cb	C	Db	D	Eb	F	Gb	Ab
Db	Eb	Fb	F	Gb	G	Ab	Bb	Cb	Db
F#	G#	A	A#	B	B#	C#	D#	E	F#
B	C#	D	D#	E	E#	F#	G#	A	B
E	F#	G	G#	A	A#	B	C#	D	E
A	B	C	C#	D	D#	E	F#	G	A
D	E	F	F#	G	G#	A	B	C	D
G	A	Bb	B	C	C#	D	E	F	G

Gypsy Minor

C	Db	E	F	G	Ab	B	C
F	Gb	A	Bb	C	Db	E	F
Bb	Cb	D	Eb	F	Gb	A	Bb
Eb	Fb	G	Ab	Bb	Cb	D	Eb
Ab	A	C	Db	Eb	Fb	G	Ab
Db	D	F	Gb	Ab	A	C	Db
F#	G	A#	B	C#	D	E#	F#
B	C	D#	E	F#	G	A#	B
E	F	G#	A	B	C	D#	E
A	Bb	C#	D	E	F	G#	A
D	Eb	F#	G	A	Bb	C#	D
G	Ab	B	C	D	Eb	F♮	G

How Did Becket - 1912 ect. -Never mind- pass on Notes taken jazz & songs
was emerging w/o ~~Notes~~ a scale & clef system - answer 1-ear 2- they
had cleff system beginning in motzar's time (period pre 1600?) - when did cleff
system arrive?

Augmented Gypsy Minor

C	D	Eb	F#	G	Ab	B	C
F	G	Ab	B	C	Db	E	F
Bb	C	Db	E	F	Gb	A	Bb
Eb	F	Gb	A	Bb	Cb	D	Eb
Ab	Bb	Cb	D	Eb	Fb	G	Ab
Db	Eb	Fb	G	Ab	A	C	Db
F#	G#	A	B#	C#	D	E#	F#
B	C#	D	E#	F#	G	A#	B
E	F#	G	A#	B	C	D#	E
A	B	C	D#	E	F	G#	A
D	E	F	G#	A	Bb	C#	D
G	A	Bb	C#	D	Eb	F#	G

Composite (1)

C	Db	Eb	E	F#	G	Ab	Bb	C
F	Gb	Ab	A	B	C	Db	Eb	F
Bb	Cb	Db	D	E	F	Gb	Ab	Bb
Eb	E	Gb	G	A	Bb	Cb	Db	Eb
Ab	A	Cb	C	D	Eb	Fb	Gb	Ab
Db	D	Fb	F	G	Ab	A	B	Db
F#	G	A	A#	B#	C#	D	E	F#
B	C	D	D#	E#	F#	G	A	B
E	F	G	G#	A#	B	C	D	E
A	Bb	C	C#	D#	E	F	G	A
D	Eb	F	F#	G#	A	Bb	C	D
G	Ab	Bb	B	C#	D	Eb	F	G

(25)

Composite (2)

C	D	Eb	F	F#	G#	A	Bb	C
F	G	Ab	Bb	B	C#	D	Eb	F
Bb	C	Db	Eb	E	F#	G	Ab	Bb
Eb	F	Gb	Ab	A	B	C	Db	Eb
Ab	Bb	Cb	Db	D	E	F	Gb	Ab
Db	Eb	Fb	Gb	G	A	Bb	Cb	Db
F#	G#	A	B	C	D	D#	E	F#
B	C#	D	E	F	G	G#	A	B
E	F#	G	A	A#	B#	C#	D	E
A	B	C	D	D#	E#	F#	G	A
D	E	F	G	G#	A#	B	C	D
G	A	Bb	C	C#	D#	E	F	G

Chord-function-scale chart

Chapter 4

The Chord–Function–Scale Chart takes the chord types as listed **(27)** and numbered in Chapter 2, relates them to their harmonic function, and assigns the most appropriate scale or scales. After you study it, you may then refer to the actual scales as presented at the end of Chapter 3.

There are many possible scales that will work over each chord type. The scales most inside the chord type are listed first with those progressively more outside following. The final scales listed in most chord types are pentatonic, blues, and exotic. Although these are not to be considered the most outside the chord type, they are listed last because of their individualistic and unique sound.

Chord	Function	Scale
1. Major Triad	I	Major—starting on root of chord Pentatonic—starting on fifth of chord Pentatonic—starting a whole step above root of chord

Chord	Function	Scale
1. Major Triad	IV	Lydian—starting on root of chord
		Pentatonic—starting on fifth of chord
		Pentatonic—starting a major sixth above root of chord
2. Minor Triad	i	Aeolian—starting on root of chord
		Melodic minor—starting on root of chord
		Harmonic minor—starting on root of chord
		Pentatonic—starting on root of chord
		Pentatonic—starting a perfect fourth above root of chord
		Augmented Gypsy Minor—starting on root of chord
2. Minor Triad	iv	Dorian—starting on root of chord
		Harmonic minor—starting on fifth of chord
		Pentatonic—starting on root of chord
		Pentatonic—starting a perfect fourth above root of chord
3. Major Sixth	I	Major—starting on root of chord
		Pentatonic—starting on root of chord
		Pentatonic—starting on fifth of chord

(28)

Chord	Function	Scale
3. Major Sixth	IV	Lydian—starting on root of chord Pentatonic—starting on fifth of chord Pentatonic—starting a major sixth above root of chord
4. Minor Sixth	i	Melodic minor—starting on root of chord Pentatonic—starting on root of chord
4. Minor Sixth	iv	Dorian—starting on root of chord Pentatonic—starting on root of chord
5. Major Seventh	I⁷	Major—starting on root of chord
5. Major Seventh	any	Lydian—starting on root of chord Pentatonic—starting a major sixth above root of chord Pentatonic—starting a whole step above root of chord
6. Major Seventh, Sharp Five	any	Melodic minor—starting a major sixth above root of chord Harmonic minor—starting a major sixth above root of chord
7. Major Seventh, Flat Five	any	Lydian—starting on root of chord Melodic minor—starting a major sixth above root of chord

(29)

Chord	Function	Scale
8. Dominant Seventh	any	Mixolydian — starting on root of chord
		Melodic minor — starting on fifth of chord
		Diminished — starting on third, fifth, or seventh of chord
		Blues — starting on root of chord
		Auxiliary blues (1 or 2) — starting on root of chord
		Pentatonic — starting on root of chord
		Pentatonic — starting a perfect fourth above root of chord
		Pentatonic — starting on fifth of chord
9. Dominant Seventh, Suspended Fourth	any	Dorian — starting on root of chord
		Dorian — starting on fourth of chord
		Dorian — starting on fifth of chord
		Dorian — starting on seventh of chord
10. Minor Seventh	i⁷, vi⁷	Aeolian — starting on root of chord
		Pentatonic — starting a perfect fourth above root of chord
		Pentatonic — starting on seventh of chord
10. Minor Seventh	ii⁷, iv⁷	Dorian — starting on root of chord
		Pentatonic — starting on root of chord
		Pentatonic — starting a perfect fourth above root of chord
		Pentatonic — starting on seventh of chord

(30)

	Chord	Function	Scale
10.	Minor Seventh	iii⁷	Phrygian — starting on root of chord Pentatonic — starting on seventh of chord
11.	Minor Triad, Major Seventh	any	Harmonic minor — starting on root of chord Augmented gypsy minor — starting on root of chord
12.	Augmented Triad	any	Whole tone — starting on root, third, or fifth of chord
13.	Dominant Seventh, Sharp Five	any	Whole tone — starting on root, third, fifth, or seventh of chord Melodic minor — starting 1/2 step above root of chord Pentatonic — starting 1/2 step above root of chord
14.	Dominant Seventh, Flat Five	any	Whole tone — starting on root, third, fifth, or seventh of chord Melodic minor — starting 1/2 step above root of chord Pentatonic — starting 1/2 step above fifth of chord (a perfect fifth above root)
15.	Half-Diminished Seventh	any	Locrian — starting on root of chord Pentatonic — starting on third of chord
16.	Diminished Triad	any	Diminished — starting on root, third, or fifth of chord Melodic minor — starting 1/2 step above root of chord Pentatonic — starting on third of chord

Chord	Function	Scale
17. Diminished Seventh	any	Diminished—starting on root, third, fifth, or seventh of chord Pentatonic—starting on third of chord Augmented gypsy minor—starting on root of chord Composite (2)—starting on root of chord
18. Major Ninth	any	Lydian—starting on root of chord Pentatonic—starting a major sixth above root of chord Pentatonic—starting a whole step above root of chord
19. Dominant Ninth	(see Dominant Seventh)	
20. Minor Ninth	(see Minor Seventh)	
21. Minor Seventh, Flat Nine	any	Phrygian—starting on root of chord Pentatonic—starting on third of chord
22. Dominant Seventh, Sharp Nine	any	Diminished—starting on third, fifth, or seventh of chord Melodic minor—starting 1/2 step above root of chord Blues—starting on root of chord Pentatonic—starting on seventh of chord Auxiliary blues (1 or 2)—starting on root of chord

(32)

Chord	Function	Scale
23. Dominant Seventh, Flat Nine	any	Diminished—starting on third, fifth, seventh, or ninth of chord Blues—starting on root of chord Melodic minor—starting 1/2 step above root of chord Pentatonic—starting on seventh of chord Gypsy minor—starting whole step above root of chord Augmented gypsy minor—starting on seventh of chord Augmented gypsy minor—starting on third of chord Composite (2)—starting on third of chord
23. Dominant Seventh, Flat Nine	V^7 in a minor key or of a minor chord	Harmonic minor—starting a perfect fourth above root of chord Composite (1)—starting on root of chord
24. Dominant Seventh, Sharp Nine, Sharp Five	any	Melodic minor—starting 1/2 step above root of chord Pentatonic—starting 1/2 step above root of chord
25. Dominant Seventh, Flat Nine, Flat Five	any	Melodic minor—starting 1/2 step above root of chord Pentatonic—starting 1/2 step above root of chord
26. Dominant Eleventh	(see Dominant Seventh)	
27. Minor Eleventh	(see Minor Seventh)	

(33)

Chord	Function	Scale
28. Major Ninth, Sharp Eleven	(see Major Seventh)	
29. Dominant Ninth, Sharp Eleven	any	Melodic minor—starting on fifth of chord Blues—starting on chord root Composite (1)—starting on root of chord
30. Dominant Seventh, Sharp Eleven, Sharp Nine	any	Diminished—starting on third, fifth, or seventh of chord Melodic minor—starting 1/2 step above root of chord Blues—starting on root of chord Pentatonic—starting on seventh of chord
31. Dominant Seventh, Sharp Eleven, Flat Nine	any	Diminished—starting on third, fifth, seventh, or ninth of chord Melodic minor—starting 1/2 step above root of chord Blues—starting on root of chord Pentatonic—starting on seventh of chord
32. Dominant Thirteenth	(see Dominant Seventh)	
33. Dominant Thirteenth, Sharp Eleven	(see Dominant Ninth, Sharp Eleven)	
34. Dominant Thirteenth, Sharp Eleven, Sharp Nine	(see Dominant Seventh, Sharp Eleven, Sharp Nine)	

Chord	Function	Scale
35. Dominant Thirteenth, Sharp Eleven, Flat Nine	(see Dominant Seventh, Sharp Eleven, Flat Nine)	
36. Dominant Thirteenth, Flat Nine	(see Dominant Seventh, Flat Nine)	
37. Quartal Three	any	Dorian — starting on root of chord Dorian — starting on fourth of chord Dorian — starting on seventh of chord Pentatonic — starting on seventh of chord
38. Quartal Four	any	Dorian — starting on root of chord Dorian — starting on fourth of chord Dorian — starting on seventh of chord Dorian — starting on tenth of chord Pentatonic — starting on tenth of chord

(35)

Scale and chord patterns on jazz scales

Chapter 5

Scale and chord patterns are presented in major, minor, and **(37)** modal settings. They are designed to aid the student in the development of technique, flexibility, and ear training.

Play each example carefully to become familiar with the scale type and its sound. Develop each example in all of its chromatic settings and relate each to its respective chord(s) and function.

Major Scale

			Pattern				
1	2	3	4	5	6	7	8
C	D	E	F	G	A	B	C
F	G	A	Bb	C	D	E	F
Bb	C	D	Eb	F	G	A	Bb
Eb	F	G	Ab	Bb	C	D	Eb
Ab	Bb	C	Db	Eb	F	G	Ab
Db	Eb	F	Gb	Ab	Bb	C	Db
F#	G#	A#	B	C#	D#	E#	F#
B	C#	D#	E	F#	G#	A#	B
E	F#	G#	A	B	C#	D#	E
A	B	C#	D	E	F#	G#	A
D	E	F#	G	A	B	C#	D
G	A	B	C	D	E	F#	G

The following scale and chord patterns are presented in the key of C Major.

1. Extend each pattern to the full range of your instrument.

2. Play each example and note the pattern involved.

3. Play each pattern in all eleven remaining keys via:
   a. Chromatic sequence (C, Db, D, Eb, etc.)
   b. Circle of fifths (C, F, Bb, Eb, etc.)
   c. Whole-step sequence
      (C, D, E, Fb, A#, B#,—B, D#, E#, F, G, A)
   d. Minor third sequence
      (C, Eb, F#, A—Bb, Db, E, G—Ab, B, D, F)

4. For improvisation purposes, major scales and patterns are used over major triads and sixth chords functioning as I. Relate each of the twelve major scales to its corresponding chords and function.

SCALE PATTERNS

(39)

INTERVALS

G# F low C#
F G C#

C G# F
Bb G E

3 G

F Minor   C G# F — 3 times
Bb G E — 1
3 twice > vice versa

(40)

CHROMATIC EMBELLISHMENT

CHORD PATTERNS   Triads

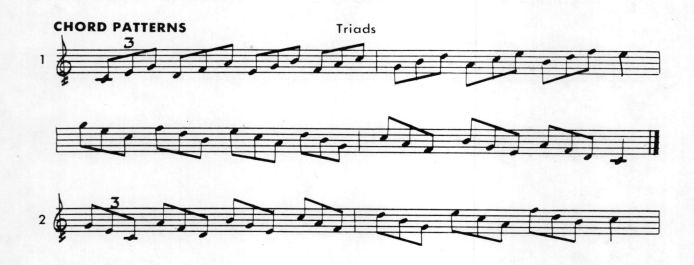

(41)

Seventh Chords

Ninth Chords

(43)

Dorian Scale

Pattern							
1	2	♭3	4	5	6	♭7	8
C	D	E♭	F	G	A	B♭	C
F	G	A♭	B♭	C	D	E♭	F
B♭	C	D♭	E♭	F	G	A♭	B♭
E♭	F	G♭	A♭	B♭	C	D♭	E♭
A♭	B♭	C♭	D♭	E♭	F	G♭	A♭
D♭	E♭	F♭	G♭	A♭	B♭	C♭	D♭
F♯	G♯	A	B	C♯	D♯	E	F♯
B	C♯	D	E	F♯	G♯	A	B
E	F♯	G	A	B	C♯	D	E
A	B	C	D	E	F♯	G	A
D	E	F	G	A	B	C	D
G	A	B♭	C	D	E	F	G

(44)

The following scale and chord patterns are presented in the key of C Dorian.

1. Extend each pattern to the full range of your instrument.

2. Play each example and note the pattern involved.

3. Play each pattern in all eleven remaining keys via chromatic sequence, circle of fifths, whole-step sequence, and minor third sequence.

4. For improvisation purposes, dorian scales and patterns are used for minor triads and sixths functioning as iv, minor seventh chords (plus any unaltered extensions) functioning as ii^7 or iv^7, sus. 4 chords or quartal chords (the scale starting on any note in the chord), and on any nonfunctional minor seventh chord. Relate each of the twelve dorian scales to its corresponding chords and function.

SCALE PATTERNS

(45)

INTERVALS

(46)

CHROMATIC EMBELLISHMENT

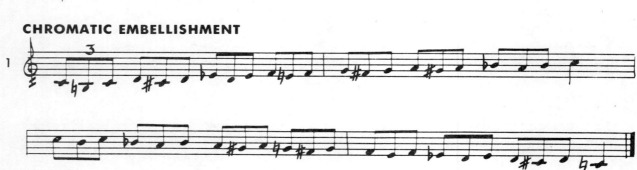

CHORD PATTERNS   Triads

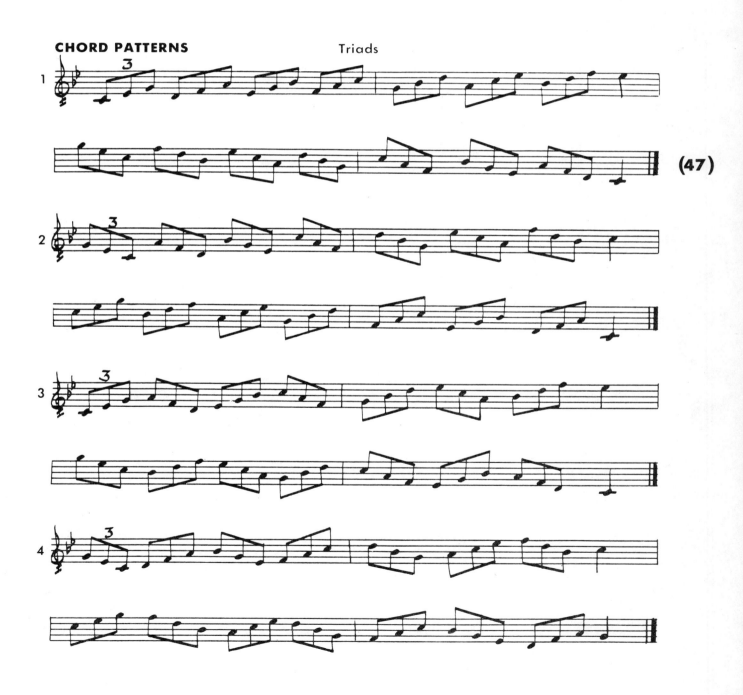

(47)

Seventh Chords

(48)

(49)

Ninth Chords

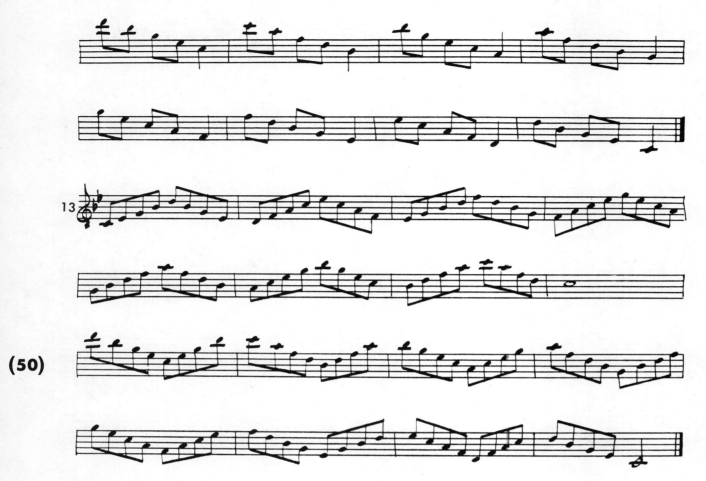

(50)

Phrygian Scale

			Pattern				
1	b2	b3	4	5	b6	b7	8
C	Db	Eb	F	G	Ab	Bb	C
F	Gb	Ab	Bb	C	Db	Eb	F
Bb	Cb	Db	Eb	F	Gb	Ab	Bb
Eb	Fb	Gb	Ab	Bb	Cb	Db	Eb
G#	A	B	C#	D#	E	F#	G#
C#	D	E	F#	G#	A	B	C#
F#	G	A	B	C#	D	E	F#
B	C	D	E	F#	G	A	B
E	F	G	A	B	C	D	E
A	Bb	C	D	E	F	G	A
D	Eb	F	G	A	Bb	C	D
G	Ab	Bb	C	D	Eb	F	G

The following scale and chord patterns are presented in the key of C Phrygian.

1. Extend each pattern to the full range of your instrument.

2. Play each example and note the pattern involved.

3. Play each pattern in all eleven remaining keys via chromatic sequence, circle of fifths, whole-step sequence, and minor third sequence.

4. For improvisation purposes, phrygian scales and patterns are used over minor seventh chords functioning as iii[7] and all minor seventh-flat nine chords. Relate each of the twelve phrygian scales to its corresponding chords and function.

SCALE PATTERNS

(51)

(52)

INTERVALS

CHROMATIC EMBELLISHMENT

CHORD PATTERNS Triads

(53)

Seventh Chords

(55)

Ninth Chords

(56)

Lydian Scale

			Pattern				
1	2	3	♯4	5	6	7	8
C	D	E	F♯	G	A	B	C
F	G	A	B	C	D	E	F
B♭	C	D	E	F	G	A	B♭
E♭	F	G	A	B♭	C	D	E♭
A♭	B♭	C	D	E♭	F	G	A♭
D♭	E♭	F	G	A♭	B♭	C	D♭
F♯	G♯	A♯	B♯	C♯	D♯	E♯	F♯
B	C♯	D♯	E♯	F♯	G♯	A♯	B
E	F♯	G♯	A♯	B	C♯	D♯	E
A	B	C♯	D♯	E	F♯	G♯	A
D	E	F♯	G♯	A	B	C♯	D
G	A	B	C♯	D	E	F♯	G

The following scale and chord patterns are presented in the key of C Lydian.

1. Extend each pattern to the full range of your instrument.

2. Play each example and note the pattern involved.

3. Play each pattern in all eleven remaining keys via chromatic sequence, circle of fifths, whole-tone sequence, and minor third sequence.

4. For improvisation purposes, lydian scales and patterns are used over major triad and sixth chords functioning as IV and for all major seventh chords.

(57)

SCALE PATTERNS

(58)

INTERVALS

(59)

CHROMATIC EMBELLISHMENT

CHORD PATTERNS Triads

(60)

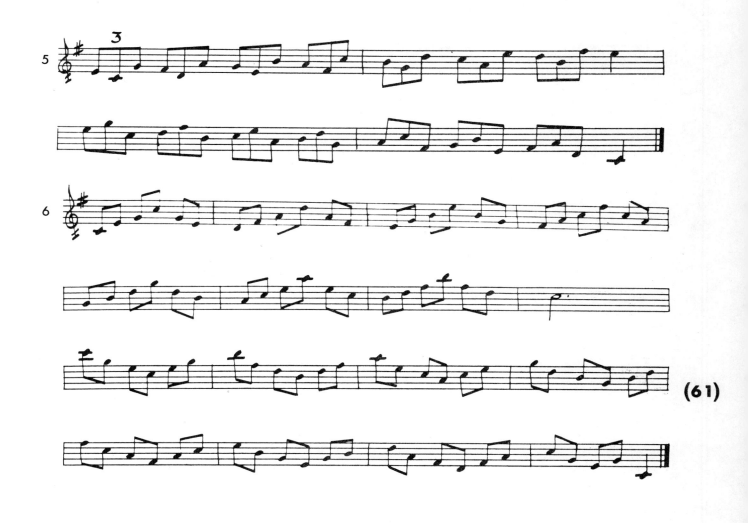

(61)

Seventh Chords

(62)

Ninth Chords

(63)

Mixolydian Scale

			Pattern				
1	2	3	4	5	6	♭7	8
C	D	E	F	G	A	B♭	C
F	G	A	B♭	C	D	E♭	F
B♭	C	D	E♭	F	G	A♭	B♭
E♭	F	G	A♭	B♭	C	D♭	E♭
A♭	B♭	C	D♭	E♭	F	G♭	A♭
D♭	E♭	F	G♭	A♭	B♭	C♭	D♭
F♯	G♯	A♯	B	C♯	D♯	E	F♯
B	C♯	D♯	E	F♯	G♯	A	B
E	F♯	G♯	A	B	C♯	D	E
A	B	C♯	D	E	F♯	G	A
D	E	F♯	G	A	B	C	D
G	A	B	C	D	E	F	G

The following scale and chord patterns are presented in the key of C Mixolydian.

1. Extend each pattern to the full range of your instrument.

2. Play each example and note the pattern involved.

3. Play each pattern in all eleven remaining keys via chromatic sequence, circle of fifths, whole-tone sequence, and minor third sequence.

4. For improvisation purposes, mixolydian scales and patterns are used over dominant seventh chords (plus any unaltered extensions) functioning as V^7.

SCALE PATTERNS

(65)

INTERVALS

CHROMATIC EMBELLISHMENT

(66)

CHORD PATTERNS

Triads

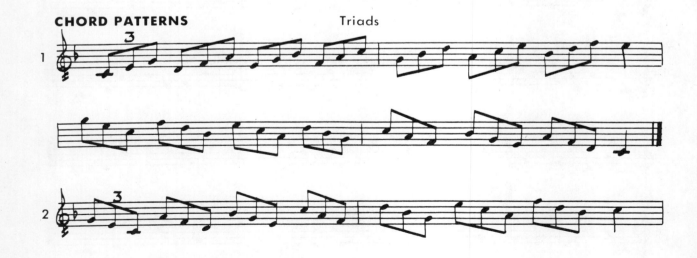

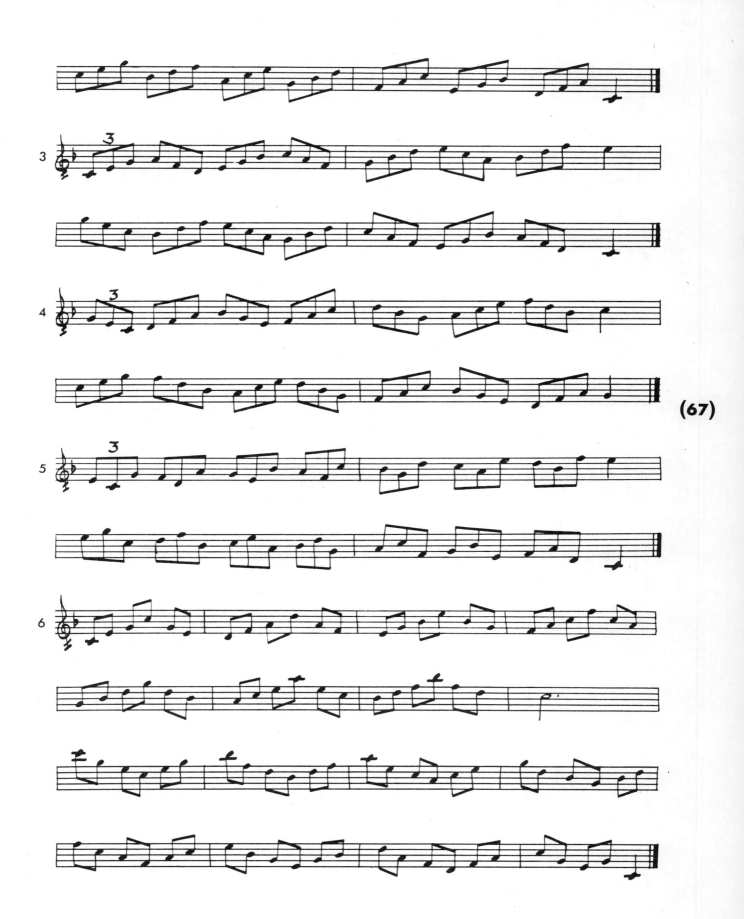

(67)

Seventh Chords

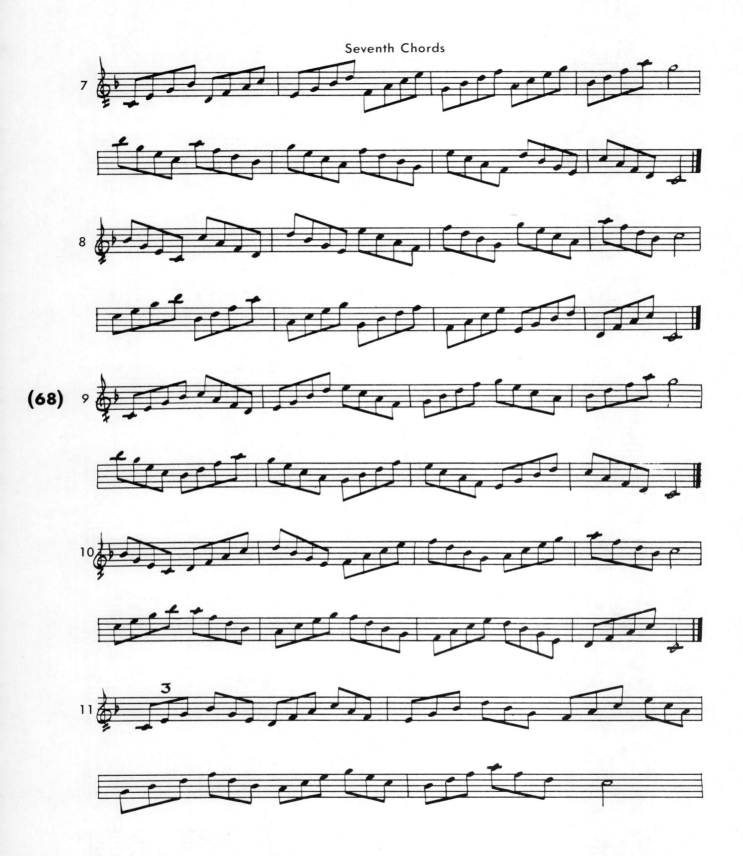

Ninth Chords

(69)

Aeolian Scale

	Pattern						
1	2	b3	4	5	b6	b7	8
C	D	Eb	F	G	Ab	Bb	C
F	G	Ab	Bb	C	Db	Eb	F
Bb	C	Db	Eb	F	Gb	Ab	Bb
Eb	F	Gb	Ab	Bb	Cb	Db	Eb
Ab	Bb	Cb	Db	Eb	Fb	Gb	Ab
C#	D#	E	F#	G#	A	B	C#
F#	G#	A	B	C#	D	E	F#
B	C#	D	E	F#	G	A	B
E	F#	G	A	B	C	D	E
A	B	C	D	E	F	G	A
D	E	F	G	A	Bb	C	D
G	A	Bb	C	D	Eb	F	G

(70)

The following scale and chord patterns are presented in the key of C Aeolian.

1. Extend each pattern to the full range of your instrument.

2. Play each example and note the pattern involved.

3. Play each pattern in all eleven remaining keys via chromatic sequence, circle of fifths, whole-step sequence, and minor third sequence.

4. For improvisation purposes, aeolian scales and patterns are used over minor triad and sixth chords functioning as i and minor seventh chords functioning as i^7 and vi^7. Relate each of the twelve aeolian scales to its corresponding chords and function.

SCALE PATTERNS

(71)

INTERVALS

CHROMATIC EMBELLISHMENT

CHORD PATTERNS

Triads

(73)

(74)

Seventh Chords

Ninth Chords

(75)

(76)

Locrian Scale

Pattern							
1	b2	b3	4	b5	b6	b7	8
C	Db	Eb	F	Gb	Ab	Bb	C
F	Gb	Ab	Bb	Cb	Db	Eb	F
Bb	Cb	Db	Eb	Fb	Gb	Ab	Bb
D#	E	F#	G#	A	B	C#	D#
G#	A	B	C#	D	E	F#	G#
C#	D	E	F#	G	A	B	C#
F#	G	A	B	C	D	E	F#
B	C	D	E	F	G	A	B
E	F	G	A	Bb	C	D	E
A	Bb	C	D	Eb	F	G	A
D	Eb	F	G	Ab	Bb	C	D
G	Ab	Bb	C	Db	Eb	F	G

The following scale and chord patterns are presented in the key of C Locrian.

1. Extend each pattern to the full range of your instrument.

2. Play each example and note the pattern involved.

3. Play each pattern in all eleven remaining keys via chromatic sequence, circle of fifths, whole-tone sequence, and minor third sequence.

4. For improvisation purposes, locrian scales and patterns are used over half-diminished seventh chords, in any function. Relate each of the twelve locrian scales to its corresponding chord.

SCALE PATTERNS

(77)

(78)

INTERVALS

CHROMATIC EMBELLISHMENT

(79)

CHORD PATTERNS

Triads

(80)

Seventh Chords

(81)

Ninth Chords

Jazz Melodic Minor Scale

Pattern							
1	2	♭3	4	5	6	7	8
C	D	E♭	F	G	A	B	C
F	G	A♭	B♭	C	D	E	F
B♭	C	D♭	E♭	F	G	A	B♭
E♭	F	G♭	A♭	B♭	C	D	E♭
A♭	B♭	C♭	D♭	E♭	F	G	A♭
C#	D#	E	F#	G#	A#	B#	C#
F#	G#	A	B	C#	D#	E#	F#
B	C#	D	E	F#	G#	A#	B
E	F#	G	A	B	C#	D#	E
A	B	C	D	E	F#	G#	A
D	E	F	G	A	B	C#	D
G	A	B♭	C	D	E	F#	G

The following scale and chord patterns are presented in the key of C Melodic Minor.

1. Extend each pattern to the full range of your instrument.

2. Play each example and note the pattern involved.

3. Play each pattern in all eleven remaining keys via chromatic sequence, circle of fifths, whole-tone sequence, and minor third sequence.

4. For improvisation purposes, melodic minor scales and patterns are used over minor triads and sixth chords that function as i, dominant seventh chords (scale starts on fifth of chord), and on dominant sevenths with any of the following alterations or extensions: ♭5, #5, ♭9, #9, or #11 (scale starts a half-step above root of chord). Relate each of the twelve melodic minor scales to its corresponding chords and function.

(83)

SCALE PATTERNS

INTERVALS

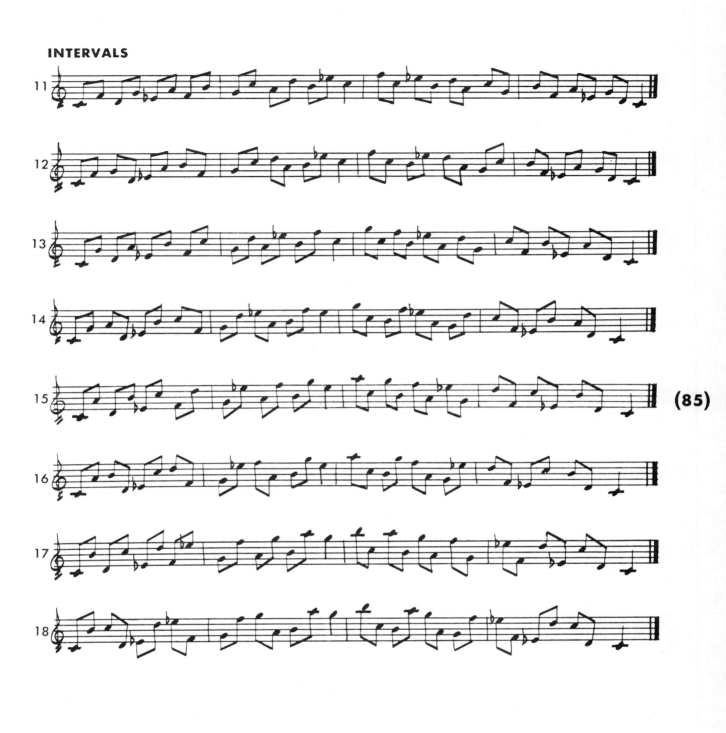

(85)

CHROMATIC EMBELLISHMENT

CHORD PATTERNS

Triads

(86)

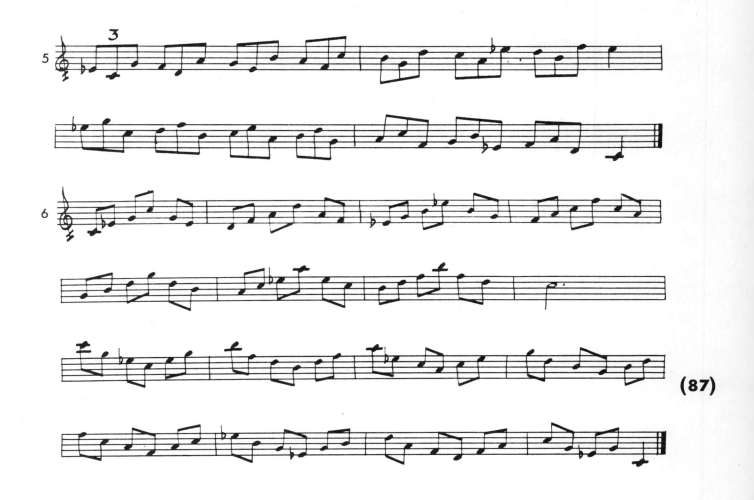

(87)

Seventh Chords

Ninth Chords

(89)

Harmonic Minor Scale

Pattern							
1	2	b3	4	5	b6	7	8
C	D	Eb	F	G	Ab	B	C
F	G	Ab	Bb	C	Db	E	F
Bb	C	Db	Eb	F	Gb	A	Bb
Eb	F	Gb	Ab	Bb	Cb	D	Eb
Ab	Bb	Cb	Db	Eb	Fb	G	Ab
C#	D#	E	F#	G#	A	B#	C#
F#	G#	A	B	C#	D	E#	F#
B	C#	D	E	F#	G	A#	B
E	F#	G	A	B	C	D#	E
A	B	C	D	E	F	G#	A
D	E	F	G	A	Bb	C#	D
G	A	Bb	C	D	Eb	F#	G

The following scale and chord patterns are presented in the key of C Harmonic Minor.

1. Extend each pattern to the full range of your instrument.

2. Play each example and note the pattern involved.

3. Play each pattern in all eleven remaining keys via chromatic sequence, circle of fifths, whole-tone sequence, and minor third sequence.

4. For improvisation purposes, harmonic minor scales and patterns are used over minor triads functioning as i, minor triads functioning as iv (scale starts on fifth of chord), minor triads with major sevenths in any function, diminished triads and diminished seventh chords in any function (scale starts a half-step above root of chord), and dominant seventh–flat nine chords functioning as V⁷ in a minor key (scale starts a fourth above root of chord). Relate each of the twelve harmonic minor scales to its corresponding chords and function.

SCALE PATTERNS

(90)

(91)

INTERVALS

CHROMATIC EMBELLISHMENT

(92)

CHORD PATTERNS   Triads

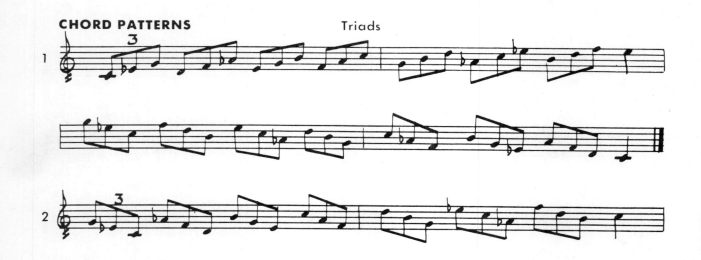

(93)

Seventh Chords

(94)

Ninth Chords

(95)

Whole-Tone Scale

			Pattern			
1	2	3	♯4	♯5	♭7	8
C	D	E	F♯	G♯	B♭	C
F	G	A	B	C♯	E♭	F
B♭	C	D	E	F♯	A♭	B♭
E♭	F	G	A	B	C♯	E♭
A♭	B♭	C	D	E	F♯	A♭
D♭	E♭	F	G	A	B	D♭
G♭	A♭	B♭	C	D	E	G♭
B	C♯	E♭	F	G	A	B
E	F♯	G♯	B♭	C	D	E
A	B	C♯	E♭	F	G	A
D	E	F♯	G♯	B♭	C	D
G	A	B	C♯	E♭	F	G

NOTE: That there are, in actuality, only two whole-tone scales.

(96)

The following scale and chord patterns are presented in the key of C Whole-Tone.

1. Note that the C whole-tone scale is the same as the D, E, F♯, A♭, and B♭ whole-tone scales.

2. Extend each pattern to the full range of your instrument.

3. Play each example and note the pattern involved.

4. Play each pattern a half-step higher to gain facility in the other whole-tone scale.

5. For improvisation purposes, whole-tone scales and patterns are used over augmented triads, dominant seventh-flat five, and dominant seventh-sharp five in any function. Relate both of the whole-tone scales to their corresponding chords and function.

SCALE PATTERNS

(97)

CHORD PATTERNS

Triads

Seventh Chords

(98)

(99)

Diminished Scale

Pattern								
1	2	♭3	4	♯4	♯5	6	7	8
C	D	E♭	F	F♯	G♯	A	B	C
F	G	A♭	B♭	B	C♯	D	E	F
B♭	C	D♭	E♭	E	F♯	G	A	B♭
E♭	F	G♭	A♭	A	B	C	D	E♭
A♭	B♭	C♭	D♭	D	E	F	G	A♭
D♭	E♭	F♭	G♭	G	A	B♭	C	D♭
F♯	G♯	A	B	C	D	E♭	F	F♯
B	C♯	D	E	F	G	A♭	B♭	B
E	F♯	G	A	B♭	C	D♭	E♭	E
A	B	C	D	E♭	F	F♯	G♯	A
D	E	F	G	A♭	B♭	B	C♯	D
G	A	B♭	C	C♯	D♯	E	F♯	G

NOTE: That there are, in actuality, only three diminished scales.

The following scale and chord patterns are presented in the key of C Diminished.

1. Note that the C diminished scale is the same as the E♭, F♯, and A diminished scales.

2. Extend each pattern to the full range of your instrument.

3. Play each example and note the pattern involved.

4. Play each pattern in the remaining two diminished tonalities.

5. For improvisation purposes, diminished scales and patterns are used over diminished triads and seventh chords in any function, dominant seventh chords and dominant seventh–flat nine or sharp nine or sharp eleven in any function (scale starts on third, fifth, or seventh of chord). Relate all three diminished scales to their corresponding chords and function.

SCALE PATTERNS

(101)

CHORD PATTERNS

Triads

1

2

(102)

3

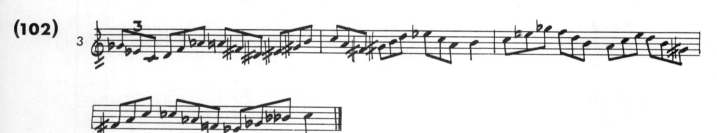

Seventh Chords

4

5

(103)

Pentatonic Scale

Pattern					
1	2	4	5	6	8
C	D	F	G	A	C
F	G	Bb	C	D	F
Bb	C	Eb	F	G	Bb
Eb	F	Ab	Bb	C	Eb
Ab	Bb	Db	Eb	F	Ab
Db	Eb	Gb	Ab	Bb	Db
F#	G#	B	C#	D#	F#
B	C#	E	F#	G#	B
E	F#	A	B	C#	E
A	B	D	E	F#	A
D	E	G	A	B	D
G	A	C	D	E	G

Scales and patterns are not presented for the pentatonic scale because the distinctive design of the scale itself supplies its most functional and widely used pattern. Each pentatonic scale should be played through the full range of your instrument and the unique pattern and sound noted.

Pentatonic scales are extremely useful in improvisation because it is possible to have a large number function for any single chord. Refer to the Chord-Function-Scale chart in Chapter 4 for a partial listing of these. Relate each of the twelve pentatonic scales to its corresponding chords and function.

Blues Scale

Pattern							
1	b3	3	4	#4	5	b7	8
C	Eb	E	F	F#	G	Bb	C
F	Ab	A	Bb	B	C	Eb	F
Bb	Db	D	Eb	E	F	Ab	Bb
Eb	Gb	G	Ab	A	Bb	Db	Eb
Ab	Cb	C	Db	D	Eb	Gb	Ab
C#	E	E#	F#	G	G#	B	C#
F#	A	A#	B	B#	C#	E	F#
B	D	D#	E	E#	F#	A	B
E	G	G#	A	A#	B	D	E
A	C	C#	D	D#	E	G	A
D	F	F#	G	G#	A	C	D
G	Bb	B	C	C#	D	F	G

Scales and patterns are not presented for the blues scale because the distinctive design of the scale itself supplies its most functional and widely used pattern. Each blues scale should be played through the full range of your instrument and the unique pattern and sound noted.

For improvisation purposes, the blues scale is used over dominant seventh chords (plus any altered or unaltered extensions) in any function. Relate each of the twelve blues scales to its corresponding chords and function.

(104)

AUXILIARY AND EXOTIC SCALES

Auxiliary Blues Scale (1)

Pattern								
1	2	b3	3	4	5	6	b7	8
C	D	Eb	E	F	G	A	Bb	C
F	G	Ab	A	Bb	C	D	Eb	F
Bb	C	Db	D	Eb	F	G	Ab	Bb
Eb	F	Gb	G	Ab	Bb	C	Db	Eb
Ab	Bb	Cb	C	Db	Eb	F	Gb	Ab
Db	Eb	Fb	F	Gb	Ab	Bb	Cb	Db
F#	G#	A	A#	B	C#	D#	E	F#
B	C#	D	D#	E	F#	G#	A	B
E	F#	G	G#	A	B	C#	D	E
A	B	C	C#	D	E	F#	G	A
D	E	F	F#	G	A	B	C	D
G	A	Bb	B	C	D	E	F	G

Scales and patterns are not presented for the auxiliary and exotic scales because the distinct design of each scale supplies its most functional and widely used pattern. Play each scale through the full range of your instrument and note the unique sound and pattern of each.

For improvisation purposes, these scales are used over dominant seventh chords (plus any altered or unaltered extensions) in any function. Relate each of these scales to its corresponding chords and function.

Auxiliary Blues Scale (2)

1	2	b3	3	4	#4	5	6	b7	8
C	D	Eb	E	F	F#	G	A	Bb	C
F	G	Ab	A	Bb	B	C	D	Eb	F
Bb	C	Db	D	Eb	E	F	G	Ab	Bb
Eb	F	Gb	G	Ab	A	Bb	C	Db	Eb
Ab	Bb	Cb	C	Db	D	Eb	F	Gb	Ab
Db	Eb	Fb	F	Gb	G	Ab	Bb	Cb	Db
F#	G#	A	A#	B	B#	C#	D#	E	F#
B	C#	D	D#	E	E#	F#	G#	A	B
E	F#	G	G#	A	A#	B	C#	D	E
A	B	C	C#	D	D#	E	F#	G	A
D	E	F	F#	G	G#	A	B	C	D
G	A	Bb	B	C	C#	D	E	F	G

(105)

Gypsy Minor

1	b2	3	4	5	b6	7	8
C	Db	E	F	G	Ab	B	C
F	Gb	A	Bb	C	Db	E	F
Bb	Cb	D	Eb	F	Gb	A	Bb
Eb	Fb	G	Ab	Bb	Cb	D	Eb
Ab	A	C	Db	Eb	Fb	G	Ab
Db	D	F	Gb	Ab	A	C	Db
F#	G	A#	B	C#	D	E#	F#
B	C	D#	E	F#	G	A#	B
E	F	G#	A	B	C	D#	E
A	Bb	C#	D	E	F	G#	A
D	Eb	F#	G	A	Bb	C#	D
G	Ab	B	C	D	Eb	F#	G

Augmented Gypsy Minor

1	2	b3	#4	5	b6	7	8
C	D	Eb	F#	G	Ab	B	C
F	G	Ab	B	C	Db	E	F
Bb	C	Db	E	F	Gb	A	Bb
Eb	F	Gb	A	Bb	Cb	D	Eb
Ab	Bb	Cb	D	Eb	Fb	G	Ab
Db	Eb	Fb	G	Ab	A	C	Db
F#	G#	A	B#	C#	D	E#	F#
B	C#	D	E#	F#	G	A#	B
E	F#	G	A#	B	C	D#	E
A	B	C	D#	E	F	G#	A
D	E	F	G#	A	Bb	C#	D
G	A	Bb	C#	D	Eb	F#	G

Composite (1)

				Pattern				
1	b2	b3	3	#4	5	b6	b7	8
C	Db	Eb	E	F#	G	Ab	Bb	C
F	Gb	Ab	A	B	C	Db	Eb	F
Bb	Cb	Db	D	E	F	Gb	Ab	Bb
Eb	E	Gb	G	A	Bb	Cb	Db	Eb
Ab	A	Cb	C	D	Eb	Fb	Gb	Ab
Db	D	Fb	F	G	Ab	A	B	Db
F#	G	A	A#	B#	C#	D	E	F#
B	C	D	D#	E#	F#	G	A	B
E	F	G	G#	A#	B	C	D	E
A	Bb	C	C#	D#	E	F	G	A
D	Eb	F	F#	G#	A	Bb	C	D
G	Ab	Bb	B	C#	D	Eb	F	G

Composite (2)

				Pattern				
1	2	b3	4	#4	#5	6	b7	8
C	D	Eb	F	F#	G#	A	Bb	C
F	G	Ab	Bb	B	C#	D	Eb	F
Bb	C	Db	Eb	E	F#	G	Ab	Bb
Eb	F	Gb	Ab	A	B	C	Db	Eb
Ab	Bb	Cb	Db	D	E	F	Gb	Ab
Db	Eb	Fb	Gb	G	A	Bb	Cb	Db
F#	G#	A	B	C	D	D#	E	F#
B	C#	D	E	F	G	G#	A	B
E	F#	G	A	A#	B#	C#	D	E
A	B	C	D	D#	Eb	F#	G	A
D	E	F	G	G#	A#	B	C	D
G	A	Bb	C	C#	D#	E	F	G

The use of nonharmonic tones

Chapter 6

Obviously, not all improvisation can be limited strictly to notes of the chord or to its allied scale forms. If this were so it is likely that improvisations would be a bit pale and lacking in excitement. Tones not indigenous to a given chord are referred to in traditional theoretical training as "nonharmonic" tones or "non-chord" tones. These terms are perhaps misleading. Nonharmonic tones play an essential role in giving spice to music. In an oversimplified sense, we can think of them as the seasoning of music, without which the food itself would be bland. Nonharmonic tones are essential to satisfactory musical structures; they should not be avoided because of their inherent dissonance. The great jazz performers utilize an instinctive ability to employ nonharmonic tones in a skillful way. Keep in mind that since jazz is an improvised art the player, although trained and benefiting from repetitious practice, still encounters a fairly large number of nonharmonic tones within any given improvisational pattern, and hence he must cultivate the ability to move quickly and be able to incorporate these tones into part of a coherent pattern, even when those tones are not part of the scale or chord form he is working around. We believe the best jazz players owe their success in part to this ability.

The basic nonharmonic tones important to the jazz musician are as follows:

Passing tones (PT)
Neighboring tones (NT)—sometimes referred to as auxiliary tones

Appoggiaturas (APP)

Escape tones (ET)—sometimes referred to as échappées

Pedal point

Let us examine each of these in turn to see how they apply to jazz patterns.

PASSING TONES

Passing tones serve the function of connecting portions of a scale pattern. For example, in Example 1 we see a CMA⁷ chord with its associated C major scale. All notes *not* belonging to the CMA⁷ chord, such as the second, fourth, and sixth (all circled here) would be classified as PTs.

EXAMPLE 1

In the context of performance, PTs may occur on either a weak beat or a strong beat, and they may be identified as either ascending or descending. If PTs are located on the weak part of the beat they are referred to as "unaccented"; if they fall on a strong beat they are referred to as "accented." The PT may be either diatonic (i.e., belonging to a scale comprised of a combination of half and whole steps as in the case of the scale in Example 1) or chromatic (including accidentals outside the stated diatonic scale structure).

Example 2 shows a diatonic improvisational pattern based on a CMA⁷ chord. Note that this pattern is a mixture of arpeggiation and conjunct (stepwise) motion. We see four PTs in this example, all in unaccented positions. Some are found in descending motion, while others are ascending.

EXAMPLE 2

Example 3, based on a Gm⁷ chord, is a bit more regular in design. Here we find a consistent pattern of triplets in which the PTs are usually located in the middle of the triplet group, in the unaccented position. The first PT, however, is found on the downbeat of the triplet and hence would be called accented.

EXAMPLE 3

Example 4, based on a Dm⁷ chord, illustrates a common sixteenth-note pattern again featuring PT in primarily unaccented positions. This pattern, however, is a bit more angular in terms of its melodic curve (the rise and fall of the melodic line).

EXAMPLE 4

Example 5, based on a G⁷ chord, illustrates the use of the chromatic PT. Note here that it is very possible to have two PTs in succession, as in the first two figures.

EXAMPLE 5

NEIGHBORING TONES Next in order of frequency of occurrence are NTs. The NT embellishes a primary chord tone by stepwise relationship also, but unlike PTs the NT figure returns to the original tone. NT may be found in ascending or descending positions. Example 6, based on the C major scale, shows an NT pattern both ascending and descending. In all cases the NT is the middle note of the three-note group.

EXAMPLE 6

If we again examine the pattern illustrated in Example 3 we see that several tones are in an NT function. Note that in Example 7 the NTs clearly do not belong to the Gm⁷ chord. Further, like passing tones, they can fall on rhythmically weak as well as on strong portions of the beat.

EXAMPLE 7

Like passing tones, neighboring tones may be chromatic as well as diatonic, as in the case of the first three NTs in Example 8.

EXAMPLE 8

A good pattern to practice—one similar to Example 6—involves the use of half-step chromatic NT embellishment of the scale, in this case C major. The pattern should, of course, be transposed to all other keys.

EXAMPLE 9

APPOGGIATURA The appoggiatura, from the Italian word *appoggiare* ("to lean"), is one of the stronger types of dissonant tones. It usually falls *on* the strong part of the beat. It is generally approached by a leap (anything larger than an intervallic second) either ascending or descending, and it resolves by stepwise motion, usually in the opposite direction. Example 10 illustrates the appoggiatura (App) in the context of a CMA⁷ chord.

EXAMPLE 10

While Example 10 shows in rather confined quarters how the appoggiatura functions, it should be noted that appoggiaturas are found less frequently than passing tones and neighboring tones.

Example 11 shows the chord progression from the jazz standard "Satin Doll" with the appoggiatura combined with PTs and NTs to illustrate how these nonharmonic tones can work in conjunction with one another. For the pianists, left-hand chord voicings are supplied here. Some are inverted forms of the basic seventh-chord structure of the tune and contain added notes to enrich the harmony as well. An additional point to make here is that the very question of whether a note is fulfilling a nonharmonic function or is being heard as a note of the extended harmonic palette (such as ninths, elevenths, and thirteenths) is often ambiguous in such a context as in Example 11. Here we have attempted to identify those nonharmonic tones that in terms of the *sound* of the example seem to fulfill a nonharmonic function most clearly.

EXAMPLE 11

ESCAPE TONE The escape tone is approached by stepwise motion and resolves via the skip, usually in the opposite direction of the approach. In Example 12 below we see the escape tone used as a dissonant factor over the first four measures of a twelve-bar blues tune in C major.

EXAMPLE 12

PEDAL POINT Pedal point is an extremely old device in music, going back hundreds of years. In concept it is a simple nonharmonic feature in which a given tone or chord is established as a constant, fixed point while harmony and melody move above it. Example 13 illustrates a pedal point G, with a series of seventh chords moving above. Some of the chords are in a more consonant relationship to the pedal point while others sound more dissonant. This is the effect the pedal gives.

EXAMPLE 13

PEDAL POINT _____→

At this point it would be wise to reiterate the point made earlier that the effective use of nonharmonic tones is critical to the improvisational performer. They must be utilized judiciously and with inventiveness in order to sound effective. Practicing patterns you invent is a must. But keep in mind that the improvisational player must anticipate that in an actual performance situation it is possible to "hear" nonharmonic features of a solo that may be new. This kind of surprise should not "throw" you, but rather should serve as a stimulus for the kind of spontaneous creation that is at the heart of inspired jazz performance.

Chromatic patterns derived from jazz scales

Chapter 7

The chromatic patterns that follow are derived from jazz scales. These patterns are more jazz-oriented than the preceding scale and chord studies, and many are extracted from solos recorded by prominent jazz artists.

Each pattern is presented in all chromatic settings. The chromatic settings of each pattern are most often achieved by chromatic ascending or descending sequence and, when more appropriate, by circles of fifths, whole-step, or minor third sequences. In any case, after working out the examples as written, you should take time to learn and play each in the remaining standard sequential patterns. This will further aid in the development of flexibility and in your ear training.

Each example presents a series of chord changes in relation to the patterns and sequence. Also indicated is the scale that matches the chord type. In many examples, alternate chord changes are presented (in parenthesis) that also fit the pattern and sequence. Please note that if these chords are used, different scales are applicable. In every instance, the alternate scales and chords also fit the examples.

There are forty-nine patterns presented here with an unlimited number of possibilities remaining. Take time to expand this list by writing down all the phrases and licks you like and transpose them to all their chromatic settings. Always relate them to the chord sequence involved and to the jazz scale utilized.

SCALE: LYDIAN (OR MAJOR OR MIXOLYDIAN)*

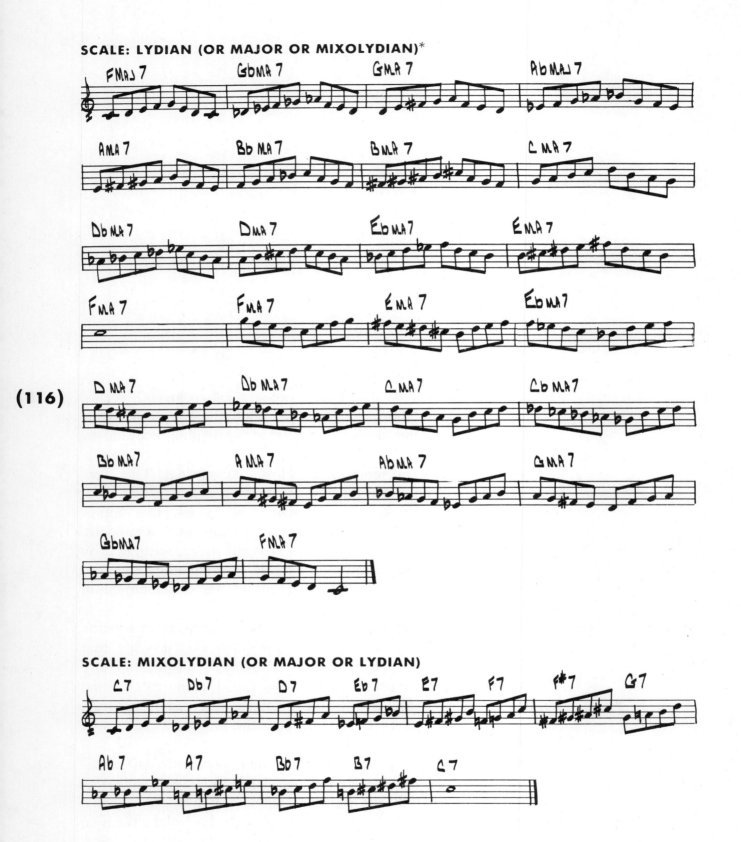

(116)

SCALE: MIXOLYDIAN (OR MAJOR OR LYDIAN)

*Chord sequence could be major beginning with C, C⁶—scale would be major, or C⁷—scale would be mixolydian, etc. Note similar situations throughout this chapter.

SCALE: MIXOLYDIAN (OR MAJOR OR LYDIAN)

SCALE: LYDIAN

(117)

SCALE: CHROMATIC

SCALE: LYDIAN

SCALE: LYDIAN

(118)

SCALE: MAJOR (OR BLUES)

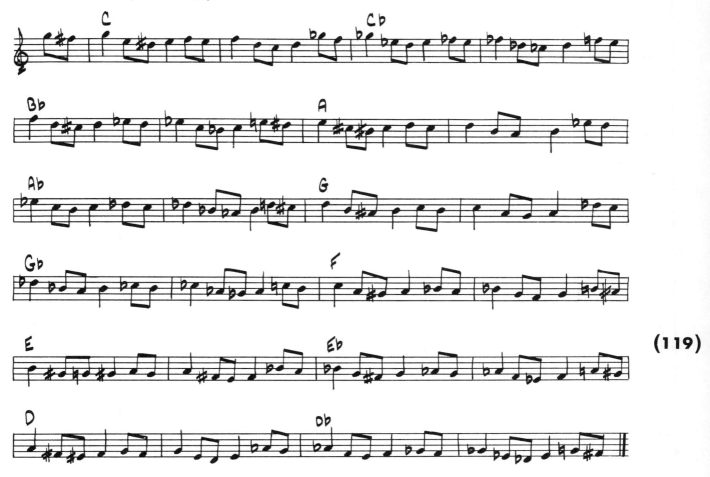

(119)

SCALE: AEOLIAN OR HARMONIC MINOR

SCALE: DORIAN OR AEOLIAN OR MELODIC MINOR
OR HARMONIC MINOR (OR LOCRIAN)

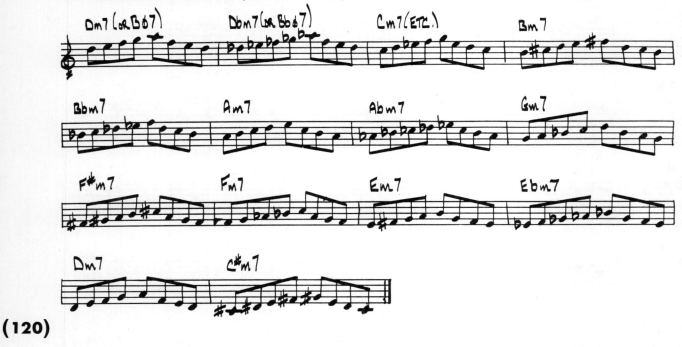

(120)

SCALE: DORIAN OR AEOLIAN OR PHRYGIAN

SCALE: PHRYGIAN

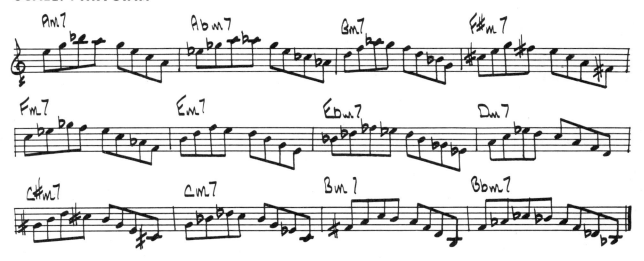

(121)

SCALE: DORIAN

SCALE: DORIAN

(122)

SCALE: DORIAN OR AEOLIAN OR PHRYGIAN

SCALE: PHRYGIAN (OR DORIAN OR MIXOLYDIAN)

(123)

SCALE: PHRYGIAN

SCALE: PENTATONIC*

SCALE: PENTATONIC

(124)

*Note that there are many chords that could be used in place of this minor seventh sequence. Only a few are listed here: sequence beginning with B♭, F, E♭, Cm, Gm, G⁷, F⁷, C⁷, Cm⁷, Gm⁷, B⁷ˣ⁵, B⁷♭⁵, Aø⁷, Ao, etc.

(125)

SCALE: CHROMATIC PATTERN—DORIAN

SCALE: CHROMATIC PATTERN-DORIAN (continued)

(126)

SCALE: MIXOLYDIAN

SCALE: CHROMATIC

(127)

SCALE: MIXOLYDIAN

SCALE: MIXOLYDIAN (continued)

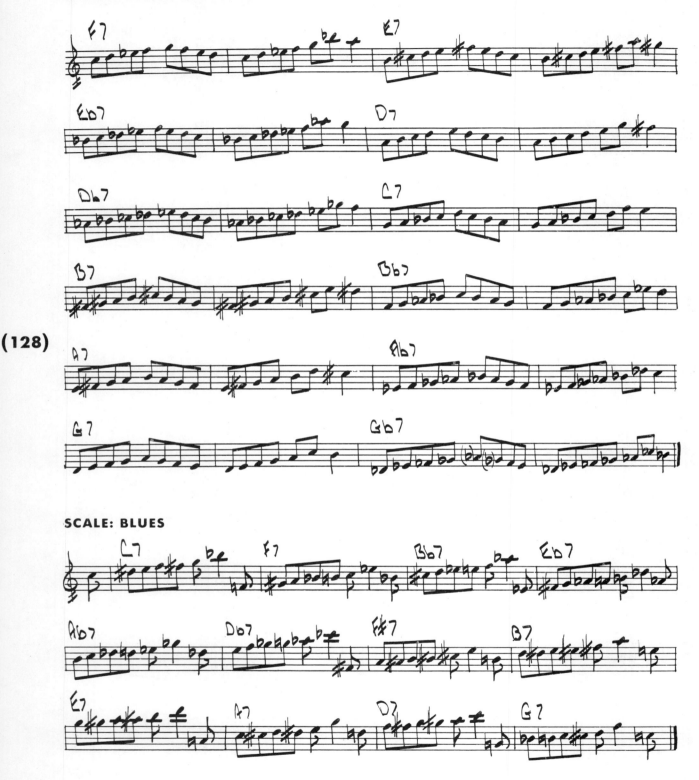

(128)

SCALE: BLUES

SCALE: MIXOLYDIAN (OR BLUES)

(129)

SCALE: MIXOLYDIAN (OR BLUES)

SCALE: MIXOLYDIAN

(130)

SCALE: MIXOLYDIAN

SCALE: MIXOLYDIAN (OR LYDIAN OR DORIAN)

(131)

SCALE: HARMONIC MINOR

SCALE: DIMINISHED

(132)

SCALE: MIXOLYDIAN

(133)

(134)

SCALE: WHOLE-TONE

C+,Bb+,Ab+,Gb+,E+,D+

B+,A+,G+,E+,Eb+,Db+,

SCALE: WHOLE-TONE

C+, Bb+,Ab+,F#+,E+,D+

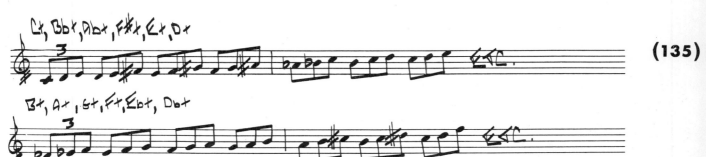

(135)

B+, A+,G+,F+,Eb+,Db+

SCALE: WHOLE-TONE

D+,E+,F#+,G#+,Bb+,C+,

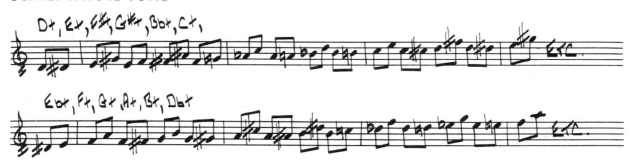

Eb+,F+,G+,A+,B+,Db+

SCALE: WHOLE-TONE

(136)

SCALE: WHOLE-TONE

SCALE: WHOLE-TONE

(137)

SCALE: DIMINISHED

SCALE: DIMINISHED

(138)

SCALE: DIMINISHED

SCALE: DIMINISHED

SCALE: DIMINISHED

(139)

SCALE: DIMINISHED

SCALE: DIMINISHED

(140)

Principles of chord voicing

Chapter 8

As a general rule all chords, regardless of type, sound best when certain voicing arrangements are followed. Let us consider, with examples, what points should be stressed regarding the voicing of chords. These principles would apply to the voicing of chords in either a keyboard or an ensemble context (e.g., arranging a chord for the saxophone section in a large jazz band).

As a general principle a chord sounds best when the largest intervallic gap is at the bottom of the chord. Furthermore, it is advised that primary members of the chord (e.g., root, fifth, seventh) *constitute the lowest interval* of the chord, in order to create a clear sense of chord identity and function. Example 1 shows five different types of seventh chords constructed on the tone C, in which each chord is governed by the interval of a seventh between the two lowest tones.

EXAMPLE 1

Sevenths can serve as the effective basis for chords until they become too low in register and begin to lose tonal clarity. Example 2 shows a descending pattern of minor seventh chords. Those marked with an asterisk become questionable as viable voicings because of their extremely low register. This is not to say that on occasion, for purposes of musical effect, these voicings would not be possible. But overall, they are too dense with overtones to be usable in most situations.

EXAMPLE 2

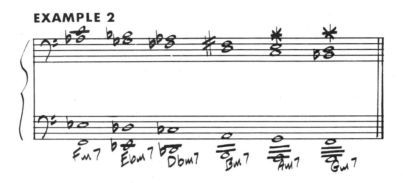

With the seventh as the dominating lower interval, chords can be voiced with more complexity than those illustrated in Example 1. The inclusion of ninths, elevenths, and thirteenths in a given chord adds to its inherent "flavor," but does not essentially alter its functional direction. That is, a plain C^7 chord has the same directional potential as a $C^7(\sharp^{11}{}_9)$, although the latter contains more tones of activity and tonal embellishment. Example 3 shows some typical chords containing added tones with the seventh as the fundamental chord pillar.

EXAMPLE 3

The perfect fifth is also quite usable as the fundamental basis for a chord. The same concern over register is still applicable, however, because fifths (or any other intervals, for that matter) tend to neutralize themselves if they get too low.

EXAMPLE 4

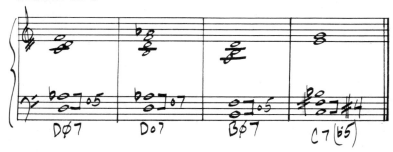

The diminished fifth can serve well as the lowest interval of either a diminished or half-diminished chord. It can also serve as the lowest interval of a dominant seventh chord containing a flatted fifth.

EXAMPLE 5

Major tenths (the third at the distance of an octave) make excellent chord foundations. Of course, for the keyboard player with a smaller hand, these may be problematic from a performance point of view.

EXAMPLE 6

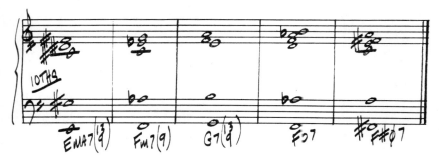

An important category of chords in today's music is the "sus. 4" chord, mentioned in an earlier chapter. Such chords are usually found to operate as substitutes for dominant seventh chords. The "sus. 4" refers to a perfect fourth suspended above the root of the chord. In classical music of the past the fourth of the chord usually was part of a 4–3 suspension figure, with the fourth ultimately resolving to the third of the chord, as in Example 7.

EXAMPLE 7

In much of the music of today the fourth does not activate to the third, but instead is "frozen" into the chord as a true chord member. The sus. 4 chord may be accurately seen as a chord of heightened dominant effect. Quite often a sus. 4 chord will be voiced in the manner illustrated below, in Example 8.

EXAMPLE 8   **EXAMPLE 9**

This fuller voicing may be analyzed as a combination of the dominant (in the bass) with the supertonic seventh chord of the key above. Here the sus. 4 element is heard as the highest pitch of the minor seventh chord above (in this case, F). This chord may also be analyzed as a $C^{7(11,\,9)}$ and in fact is occasionally indicated that way. Note that the eleventh in this case would be a perfect eleventh in relation to the root of the chord, not an augmented eleventh, which perhaps is the more common form of the eleventh to be found above a dominant seventh chord. In addition, it is important to remember that if the chord is indicated in this fashion one should not utilize the third of the chord, because this would conflict with the sus. 4 feeling granted by the eleventh above. In Example 9 we' see another common form of the same chord.

Here a B♭ major seventh chord is placed above the dominant octave. In fact this chord sounds much like the Gm⁷ chord, with the exception that the B♭ major seventh chord has the tone A as a chord member minus the G. The principle then for constructing this fuller voicing of the sus. 4 chord is to superimpose a major seventh chord a minor seventh above the dominant.

This brings us to the subject of inversions or chords *not* in root position. Perhaps the first step for the jazz player would be to learn the inversions of all basic triads and seventh chords before proceeding to more complex inversions. A word is in order here concerning a major difference between chord construction as handled in "classical" music theory and jazz. In classical music, triads and seventh chords are indicated in a system known as the figured bass. Here, both Roman numerals and arabic figures indicate (1) the designation of the chord in terms of the parent key and (2) the precise intervallic organization above the root of the chord. Example 10 shows the sequence of triads in the key of G major and Example 11 illustrates the same triads enhanced by one more note so as to form seventh chords.

EXAMPLE 10

EXAMPLE 11

The large Roman numerals indicate that the triad is major while small numerals indicate minor triads or diminished triads if the chord is followed by a o or ø. This system of chord nomenclature, then, relates chords to a key in a hierarchical manner.

To invert these chords, the same Roman numeral would be retained, but the inversion is indicated as shown in Example (12) below.

EXAMPLE 12

The parentheses around Arabic numerals indicate that often that figure is dropped from the chord indication, even though it obviously specifies a chord member. This is done because of convention and for ease of writing.

Now, the jazz system of chord nomenclature does not employ these Roman and Arabic figures. Instead, each chord is indicated by its root name and quality type. Example 13 illustrates how jazz musicians would indicate these chords.

EXAMPLE 13

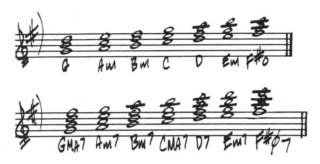

When we then tackle the problem of inversions in regard to jazz chords we find that the system indicates, instead of the intervallic construction above the root, *the chord quality and the pitch serving as lowest member.* For example, the seventh chords shown in Example (14) would be indicated in either of two ways in the jazz system:

EXAMPLE 14

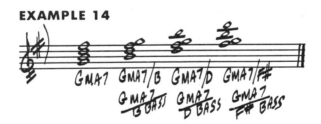

The possibilities for specific inversion chord voicings are many, and no one chart can possibly indicate all of them. Let's take one chord type at a time and explore some of the possibilities available for inversion voicings. If we study a dominant seventh structure we will find that the greatest amount of tonal variety may be elicited by this chord. Hence, we have the richest palette available with this particular chord type. Example 15 illustrates eight possibilities for first inversions of a C^7 chord, enhanced by ninths, elevenths, and thirteenths on occasion.

EXAMPLE 15

$C7/E$ $C7/E$ $C7(b9)/E$ $C7(#9)/E$ $C7#5/E$ $C7#5/E$ $Cb69/E$ $C7b6/E$ $C7(#11)/E$

The numbers beside the chord indicate the precise constitution of the chord in terms of tone members. Other tone complexes would be possible in the treble clef, but these have been kept the same in each example so we can focus on the main part of the inverted chord in the bass clef. All of these first-inversion voicings should be *played* at the keyboard so you can hear the differences between them. Every musician will have his or her personal preferences when it comes to voicings. Hence, it is important to be as familiar as possible with the different variants in order to establish a basic repertoire.

We next move to voicings containing the fifth in the bass. These are fewer in number than those illustrated in Example 15 because there we saw that the tone of the chord was easily generated with the third in the bass. The notes appearing in the treble clef have also been varied here so that the inversion voicing below will be complemented well.

EXAMPLE 16

$C7(13)/G$ $C7(9)/G$ $C7(13)/G$ $C7(b9)/G$ $C7(sus4)/G$ $C7(b9)/G$ $C7(b9)/G$

Finally, in Example 17 we have the third inversion voicings with the original seventh of the chord as the lowest note. Here again, as with the first-inversion chords, we have a tritone member as the basic low note so as to offer a rather automatic dominant feeling if the third is used above the seventh.

EXAMPLE 17

(149)

Common jazz chord progressions

Chapter 9

CIRCLE(CYCLE) OF FIFTHS

There is no chord movement in tonal music more powerful than that found between two chords related by root movement up an intervallic perfect fourth or down a perfect fifth. This cycle, when carried through all twelve tones of the scale, yields the following pattern:

EXAMPLE 1

a)

Up by perfect fourths

b)

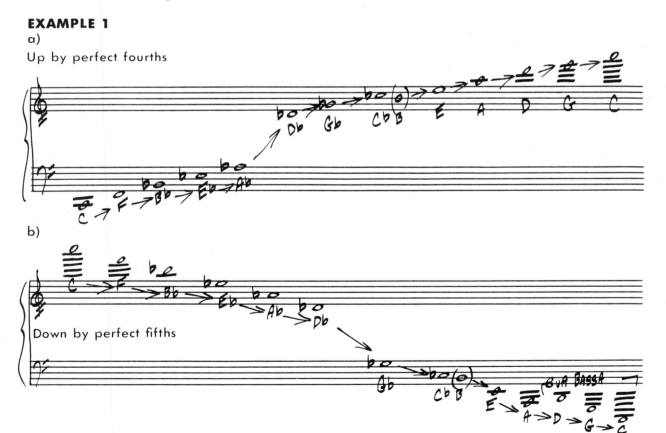

Down by perfect fifths

Put into schematic form, as it is most often seen, the cycle then would appear as seen below:

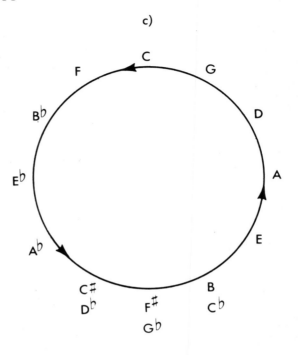

c)

Certain theorists, such as Richard Franko Goldman in his book *Harmony in Western Music**, present a compelling case for the primacy of this pattern as the underlying foundation beneath all harmonic progression and design. Even though a particular progression may deviate from the cycle at a given point it almost always will revert to the cycle for cadential purposes. The cycle is often seen in jazz progressions as a chain of dominant seventh chords such as $C^7 - F^7 - Bb^7 - Eb^7$ etc. Many older standard tunes in particular utilize this model as the primary basis for chordal movement. Or, the cycle may manifest itself in terms of the ii-V-I progression where the chord quality changes (minor seventh to dominant seventh to major seventh). In much jazz of the 1970s the dominant impulse is avoided altogether, and one might encounter a progression such as $Cm^7 - Fm^7 - Bbm^7$, which has a modal flavor. Perhaps it would be best to state rather unequivocally that, given root movement of the cycle of fifths, any chord quality may then be applied to retain the strong forward motion inherent in the cycle. Let us take the roots C, F, and Bb and experiment with different chordal qualities upon these roots. Example 2(a) illustrates the C — F — Bb cycle with dominant seventh quality of each chord. Examples 2(b) and 2(c) contain chord embellishments in the form of added ninths, elevenths, and

*Richard Franko Goldman, *Harmony in Western Music* (New York: W. W. Norton & Co., 1965).

thirteenths. Regardless of the type of coloristic addition, the basic flavor of the pattern is the same, dominated by the pattern of cycle root movement.

EXAMPLE 2

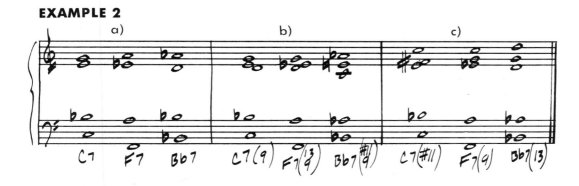

Examples 3(a), 3(b), and 3(c) show a sequence of major seventh chords on the same roots. As with those found above, Examples 3(b) and 3(c) present, in particular, the major seventh chords with more complicated embellishments.

(153)

EXAMPLE 3

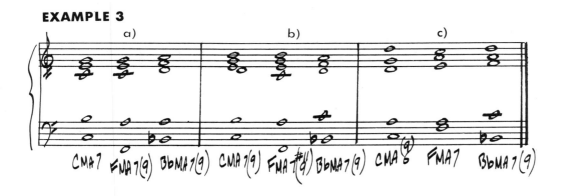

Examples 4(a), 4(b), and 4(c) are limited to minor seventh chordal quality, again with some of the chords containing additions to enhance the color of the overall progression.

EXAMPLE 4

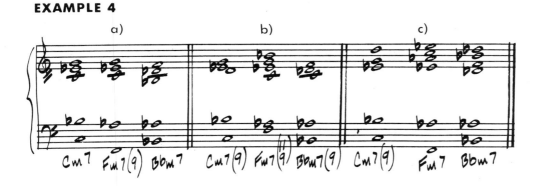

The sets of mixed chord types appear in Examples 5 through 15. Here different sequences have been incorporated because each example makes use of a different quality order. Example 5 is the standard minor seventh–dominant seventh–major seventh sequence so common to jazz of every variety.

EXAMPLE 5

Example 6 is similar to 5, but substitutes a half-diminished chord in place of the minor seventh chord.

EXAMPLE 6   **EXAMPLE 7**

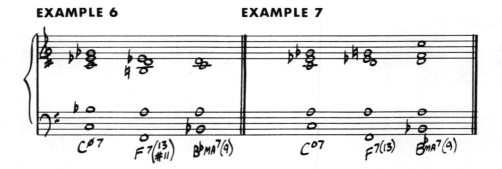

Example 7 places a fully diminished seventh chord leading to the dominant. This chordal pattern sounds less successful in terms of the forward "drive." The Gb in the first chord actually has an upward tendency to the G♮ of the second chord.

Example 8 might be considered to constitute a double supertonic motion to the dominant in that two minor seventh chords precede the Bb⁷ chord.

EXAMPLE 8

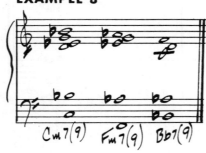

Example 9 is a reversal of Example 8 in that the dominant moves to the minor seventh chord — a retrogression, so to speak, compared to Example 8.

EXAMPLE 9

Example 10 shows the half-diminished chord — an equivocal type of chord moving into a dominant seventh, as it often does in functional jazz settings.

EXAMPLE 10

Example 11 illustrates the use of another rather equivocal chord, the diminished seventh, resolving (in what might be considered a more irregular resolution) to a dominant seventh chord on the root a perfect fifth down from F.

EXAMPLE 11

Example 12 shows two major seventh chords moving into a dominant seventh chord.

EXAMPLE 12

Example 13 illustrates three diminished seventh chords in succession. It is often pointed out that in jazz the diminished seventh chord most often serves as a chord of stepwise connection between two other more primary chords. This is not the case here.

(156)

EXAMPLE 13

In Example 14 we see a pattern common to many jazz pieces—that of a major seventh chord moving into a minor seventh chord which in turn moves into a dominant chord.

EXAMPLE 14

Example 15 is similar to 14, except that here the dominant seventh chord precedes the major and minor seventh chords.

EXAMPLE 15

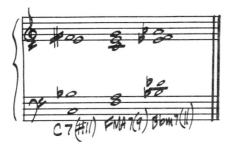

Example 16 illustrates the use of the suspended fourth chord (sus. 4), a chord common to much jazz and popular music after 1968.

EXAMPLE 16

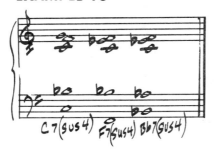

THE II–V–I PROGRESSION

There is no more important progression in jazz than the ii–V–I progression. It permeates, to a greater or lesser degree, almost all popular songs or "standards" used as vehicles for improvisation as well as many forms of blues progressions.

The designation by Roman numerals merely indicates the position of the root of the chord in terms of a given major or minor scale. For example, in the key of G major the second scale degree is A, the fifth is D, and the first is G. The ii–V–I progression in any key is based upon three essentially different chord types. The ii chord is minor in triadic quality; the V chord is major, as is the I chord. However, in jazz these chords are almost always utilized as seventh chords. Hence the ii^7 chord would be the minor seventh type, V^7 would constitute the dominant factor, while I^7 would be a major seventh chord. Example 17 (a) illustrates a triadic ii–V–I progression. Example 17 (b) shows a ii^7–V^7–I^7 progression in the same key.

EXAMPLE 17

The three basic chord types have essentially different functions in the context of the ii–V–I progression. The supertonic (ii) minor seventh chord serves as a "feeder" chord to the dominant (V) seventh chord. The dominant seventh chord is a chord of activity with a strong need for resolution. Most often it resolves to a tonic (I) chord; in the case above, it resolves to a major seventh chord, which serves as a chord of repose or cadential function. Many jazz tunes present harmonic layouts formulated around sequential ii–V–I patterns, each "tonic" chord forming a relationship to other, following ii–V–I patterns. We shall shortly see how such chord sequences operate and are linked together. Utilizing chord symbols, we can now postulate the ii^7–V^7–I^7 progression in every key:

(158)

C Major:	Dm^7	G^7	CMA^7
D♭ Major:	$E♭m^7$	$A♭^7$	$D♭MA^7$
D Major:	Em^7	A^7	DMA^7
E♭ Major:	Fm^7	$B♭^7$	$E♭MA^7$
E Major:	$F♯m^7$	B^7	EMA^7
F Major:	Gm^7	C^7	FMA^7
G♭ Major:	$A♭m^7$	$D♭^7$	$G♭MA^7$
G Major:	Am^7	D^7	GMA^7
A♭ Major:	$B♭m^7$	$E♭^7$	$A♭MA^7$
A Major:	Bm^7	E^7	AMA^7
B♭ Major:	Cm^7	F^7	$B♭MA^7$
B Major:	$C♯m^7$	$F♯^7$	BMA^7

At this point it is important to discuss some of the basic chord substitutions and additions that occur frequently in the context of the ii–V–I progression. The chord most closely allied to the supertonic chord is the half-diminished chord. Indeed, it is easy to see how these two are related, because there proves to be only one different note, the fifth, when the two are compared. Since the fifth is lowered by a half-step in the half-diminished seventh chord, we can see that a diminished triad results, as compared to the minor triad of the minor seventh chord. This also means that the interval between the root of the chord and the fifth constitutes a diminished fifth in the half-diminished seventh chord, as opposed to a perfect fifth in the minor seventh chord. The diminished fifth is more intervallically charged than the perfect fifth; and this fact holds implications for the voice-leading in the resolution of this chord, which we shall discuss later. Example 18 lists all of the minor seventh chords followed by their variant half-diminished brethren.

EXAMPLE 18

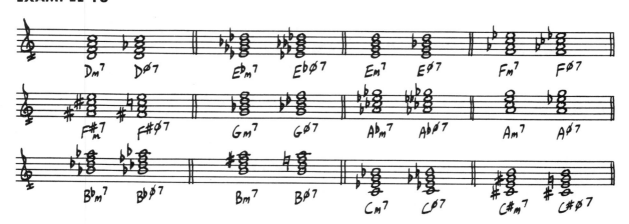

(159)

It should be noted that we advocate in this book the use of the half-diminished sign (ø) to replace the system of indicating this chord as m7b5. The latter seems unnecessarily complicated, although the reader should be well aware of it since it is in use quite predominantly. The sign (ø) is quite commonly taught in traditional theory courses, and it seems to be a handy way to indicate this chord in jazz also.

In terms of actual jazz tunes, then, the half-diminished chord may supplant the minor seventh chord as it moves to the dominant. It is interesting to observe that jazz pieces in minor keys seem to employ the half-diminished chord more than the minor seventh chord in the supertonic function. The reason for this seems clear. Given the fact that the natural minor scale as well as the harmonic minor scale contains a lowered sixth scale degree, this in turn becomes the lowered fifth of the ii chord, as illustrated in Example 19.

EXAMPLE 19

The outstanding characteristic of the dominant seventh chord is the tritone interval located between its third and seventh degrees. This tritone is the "active ingredient" that has such a strong propensity to resolve to tonic. Example 20 shows the tritone of a D^7 chord resolving to primary notes (root and third) of the tonic chord. If the tritone is utilized as a diminished fifth, it typically resolves inward; if it is used as an augmented fourth, it tends to resolve outward.

EXAMPLE 20

Now, the same tritone occurs in dominant chords related to one another by the tritone root interval also. That is, a D^7 chord contains the same tritone as that of an $A\flat^7$ chord, although the pitches are spelled differently.

EXAMPLE 21

Although the C–G♭ tritone would normally resolve to the pitches D♭ and F in a D♭ chord, it can also be heard in a dominant function moving to the notes of a GMA⁷ chord. This means, then, that we may now postulate the following substitute pairs for dominant seventh chords:

$G^7–D\flat^7$	$B^7–F^7$	$E\flat^7–A^7$
$A\flat–D^7$	$C^7–G\flat^7$	$E^7–B\flat^7$
$A^7–E\flat^7$	$D\flat^7–G^7$	$F^7–B^7$
$B\flat^7–E^7$	$D^7–A\flat^7$	$F\sharp^7–C^7$

In jazz, the tritone root substitution most often takes place as a form of parallel chord movement. For example, we see that in the standard ii–V–I progression in G Major all of the chords are related by fifths: A–D–G. If an $A\flat^7$ chord is substituted for the D^7, we then get a chromatic stepwise parallel chord movement: A–A$\flat$–G. We can, at this point, generalize and say that any dominant seventh chord moving to its corresponding tonic may be substituted for by the chord a tritone away, thus creating a descending pattern of half-steps. Example 22 below illustrates a contextual substitution of an $A\flat^7$ chord for a D^7 chord.

EXAMPLE 22

(161)

Am7   Ab7   GMA7

The third category of basic substitutions has to deal with the tonic chord. Depending on the mode (major or minor) and the setting, certain basic substitutions may be utilized. These are as follows:

a. For a major seventh chord the major sixth chord may serve.
b. In minor keys the minor sixth chord or the minor/major seventh chord may be utilized.

Example 23 illustrates these chords on the root G.

EXAMPLE 23

GMA7   GMA6   Gm6   GmMA7

Example 24 below is an example of a ii–V–I progression in the minor mode utilizing the chord types discussed above.

Example 25, in F minor, utilizes the half-diminished supertonic, the dominant substitution moving down by half-step to the tonic minor/major seventh chord.

EXAMPLE 24

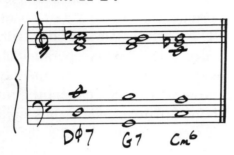

EXAMPLE 25

Seventh Chord Type	Common extensions	Less common extensions
Major Seventh	a. Major Ninth b. Augmented Eleventh	a. Major Thirteenth
Dominant Seventh	a. Major Ninth b. Minor Ninth c. Augmented Ninth d. Perfect Eleventh e. Augmented Eleventh f. Major Thirteenth	a. Minor Thirteenth
Minor Seventh	a. Major Ninth b. Perfect Eleventh c. Major Thirteenth	a. Minor Ninth b. Augmented Eleventh c. Minor Thirteenth
Half-diminished seventh	a. Minor Ninth b. Perfect Eleventh	
Diminished Seventh	(none)	a. Major Seventh b. Major Ninth c. Perfect Eleventh d. Minor Thirteenth
Dominant Seventh— sharp five	a. Augmented Ninth	a. Minor Ninth
Dominant Seventh— flat five	a. Minor Ninth	a. Augmented Ninth
Dominant Seventh— sus. four	a. Major Ninth	a. Major Thirteenth
Minor Triad— Major Seventh	a. Major Ninth	

At this point we should consider some of the basic chord extensions to the essential seventh chords of the $ii^7 – V^7 – I^7$ sequence. Any seventh chord may be enhanced through the utilization of added ninths, elevenths, and thirteenths. We can further specify that some additions are quite common, while others are found with less frequency. The following chart lists the possible extensions to each of the chord types common to the ii–V–I sequence.

It is readily apparent that the greatest number of extensions apply to the dominant seventh chord. This is indeed fortunate, for a chord that has such a critical "activity" function can then be enhanced in any number of ways. It should also be stressed at this point that jazz almost never employs a plain dominant seventh chord. While the minor seventh chord, major seventh chord, half-diminished seventh chord, and diminished seventh chord can stand by themselves quite well, the dominant seventh chord, in order to sound stylistically appropriate, needs to be enhanced through the utilization of chord extensions.

Example 26 illustrates the use of added ninths on all three chords. Note that the ninth of the dominant chord is first heard as the fifth of the minor seventh chord, creating a common tone connection between the two sonorities.

(163)

Example 27 illustrates the use of added elevenths. These may occur with or without the ninths present, depending on the need for harmonic density and complexity.

EXAMPLE 26

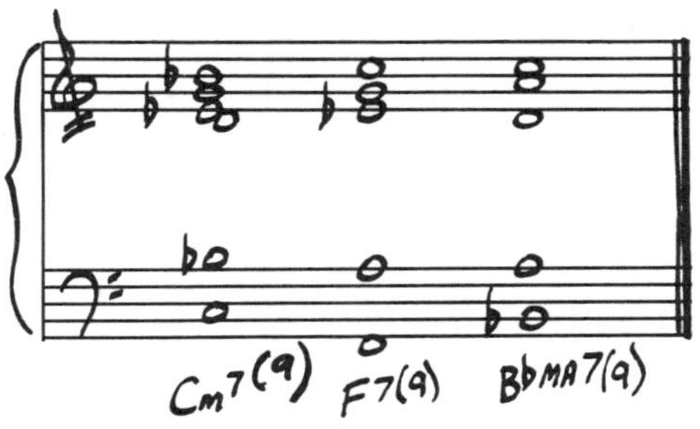

EXAMPLE 27

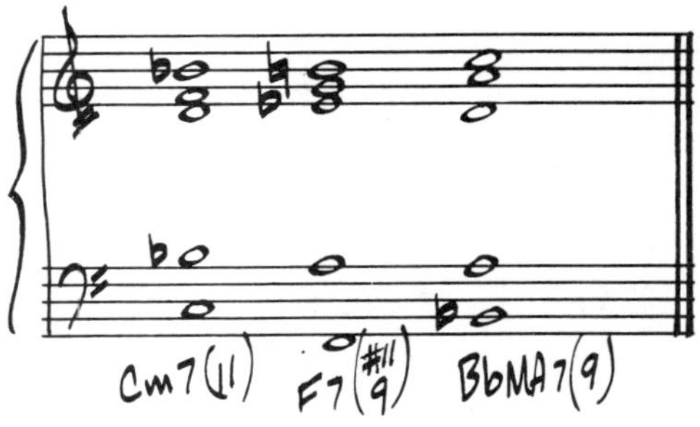

Example 28 illustrates the use of added thirteenths. It should be noted that the major thirteenth is equivalent to a major sixth above the root at the distance of an octave. Hence, the thirteenth may on occasion be indicated as an added sixth. This is particularly true in the case of major seventh chords and dominant seventh chords. For example, the symbol $B\flat^{7/6}$ would indicate a $B\flat$ dominant seventh chord with an added thirteenth.

EXAMPLE 28

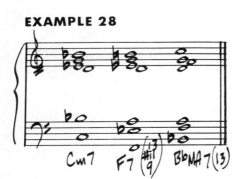

In a similar fashion the dominant seventh chord with the augmented and flatted fifth functions in effect the same as the chord extended by a lowered thirteenth and augmented eleventh. For example, $C^{7\,(\sharp 5)}$ and $C^{7\,(\flat 5)} = C^{7\,(\sharp 11)}$.

THE TURNAROUND

The turnaround is a harmonic sequence employed at the end of a jazz piece that leads back into the start of the tune. Very often it constitutes a more complicated chordal pattern that is meant to supplant a static chord such as the dominant or tonic that would otherwise be sustained over many beats at the end of the piece. The experienced jazz player should have several different turnaround combinations at his or her command so as to be able to easily facilitate an effective recycling of the tune. The basic cycle of fifths usually supplies the motivating harmonic drive for a typical turnaround sequence. If, for example, we were to encounter the harmonic sequence outlined in Example 29 below it would be more or less assumed that the player would strive to enhance this pattern via a more active harmonic rhythm.

EXAMPLE 29

Example 30 illustrates one of the most common substitution sets. Here we see that after the first chord (the tonic) the E⁷, A⁷, and D⁷ chords are related by the all-powerful fifth root movement. Also, in terms of chord type all of the chords except the first one are dominant sevenths, probably the most active of all chords.

EXAMPLE 30

Example 31 retains the same root movement of the preceding example. The main difference here is that instead of an E⁷ chord we find a minor seventh chord on E and likewise an Am⁷ chord instead of the A⁷ of Example 30. It should be noted that many of the chords in these turnarounds have been enhanced with various combinations of ninths, elevenths, and thirteenths. Many types of ninths, elevenths, and thirteenths can be employed, and the ones found here are by no means the *only* version of chordal embellishment that will work in the context of the turnaround. Indeed, each player should strive to experiment with many different chord tones above the given basic pattern of the turnaround in question.

(165)

EXAMPLE 31

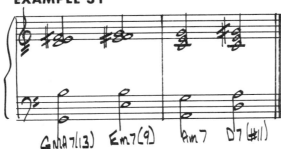

Example 32 mixes the dominant seventh and minor seventh chords in a slightly new order. And, of great importance here is the substitution of a Bm⁷ chord for the tonic GMA⁷ as the first chord of the turnaround. The inclusion of Bm⁷ now relates all of the chord roots by fifths (B→E→A→D). A basic principle illustrated here is that a minor seventh chord (e.g., Bm⁷) a major third above the root of the tonic chord can be effectively employed as a substitution for the tonic. This avoids the finality of the tonic chord, and has the effect of moving the turnaround ahead.

EXAMPLE 32

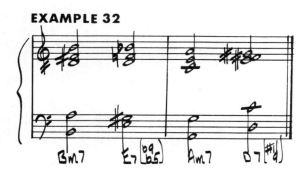

Example 33 shows three chords related by half-step root movement. The Em⁷ chord, instead of progressing to the A⁷ chord, moves stepwise to an E♭⁷ chord. As was pointed out in the section on ii–V–I, two dominant seventh chords a tritone apart contain the same internal tritone. Hence, in Example 34 we see that E♭⁷, which replaces A⁷, contains the same tritone (G–D♭) as the A⁷ chord (G–C♯). This fact makes these chords brothers of a sort, with important substitution possibilities resulting from the tritone similarity. The E♭⁷ chord then progresses stepwise to the dominant chord, completing the chain of conjunct root movement.

EXAMPLE 33

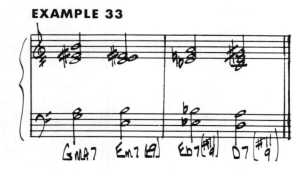

Example 34 again contains the half-step root pattern, but generated from a different source. The principle of tritone similarity mentioned earlier becomes very apparent here, because we can readily see that the B♭⁷ chord would be interchangeable with an E⁷ chord; the A⁷ chord is interchangeable with an E♭⁷ chord, and the A♭⁷ chord is interchangeable with a D⁷ chord. The pattern in Example 34 moves from a B♭⁷ source in downward motion, giving us a situation involving the I–♭III–II–♭II configuration.

EXAMPLE 34

Example 35 starts out as did Example 34, with a G to B♭⁷ motion. However, we then see the reappearance of fifth-root movement (B♭–E♭–A♭), with the chords in measure 2 being of the major seventh variety instead of the more common minor sevenths and dominant sevenths of the preceding examples. The sound of major seventh chords used in this fashion can be a refreshing change in a turnaround.

EXAMPLE 35

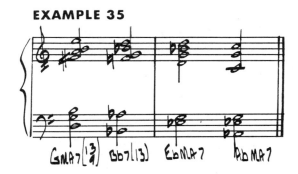

Example 36 illustrates the passing diminished seventh chord (G♯°⁷) moving between the tonic and the Am⁷ chord. This is probably the most common setting for a diminished seventh chord in jazz. Also, this causes the first three chords to be related again by half-step root movement, with the difference that in this situation we see an ascending instead of a descending bass motion.

EXAMPLE 36

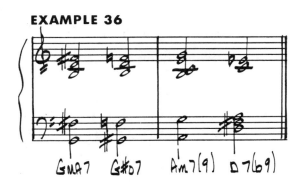

Example 37 illustrates a slightly different utilization of the major seventh chord, because a descending motion from G to D is colored by major seventh chords on G, F, and E♭. The dominant on D remains, although it would be possible to make the D⁷ chord a major seventh chord as well.

EXAMPLE 37

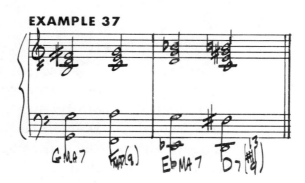

Example 38 begins, as did Example 37, with a stepwise motion down from G to F. This time, however, the F chord is dominant instead of major seventh in quality. This particular turnaround has a rather symmetrical design in that it is framed by two whole-step descending root movements (G–F and B♭–A♭) while the internal root movement of F–B♭ is cycle-of-fifths oriented.

EXAMPLE 38

Perhaps no other chord has characterized jazz of the last ten years—particularly so-called "funky" jazz—more than the augmented ninth chord. In reality this chord achieves its "bite" via the juxtaposition of the major third and the minor third (voiced as an augmented ninth above the chord root). In this chord we have the true mingling of the major and minor modes so common to the quality of a blues third. The turnaround in Example 39 shows a sequencing of augmented ninth chords moving in descending parallel progression.

EXAMPLE 39

Example 40 is, again, cycle-of-fifths-oriented with regard to the first three chords. The movement from F⁷–D⁷, however, constitutes a descending minor third. Note also how the chord qualities are aligned differently here; we see two major seventh sonorities followed by two dominant seventh sonorities.

EXAMPLE 40

Example 41 is a bit more complex than the preceding patterns in that it has a more active quality in the first measure, with a stepwise passing chord pattern from GMA⁷ up to B♭⁷. From B♭⁷ down to A♭⁷ we see much the same type of stepwise root movement illustrated earlier. A turnaround such as this one might be more easily and effectively employed in a piece with a slower tempo.

EXAMPLE 41

Major seventh sonorities again appear as the first three chords of Example 42, followed by a tritone skip from the AbMA⁷ chord down to the D⁷ chord. As we have seen earlier, these latter two chords are not quite as far removed from one another as might first appear. However, note here that the Ab chord is major in quality, not dominant, so that the tritone commonality we spoke of earlier is not present here.

EXAMPLE 42

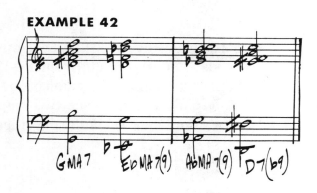

GMA7   EbMA7(9)   AbMA7(9)   D7(b9)

(170)

JAZZ LINES UTILIZING COMMON PROGRES-SIONS

Following are eighteen jazz patterns highlighting various ii–V–I, circle-of-fifths patterns, and turnaround progressions. Again they are presented in every key and in the most appropriate sequential pattern. There are an endless number of patterns possible and the eighteen presented here serve only to illustrate some of these possibilities.

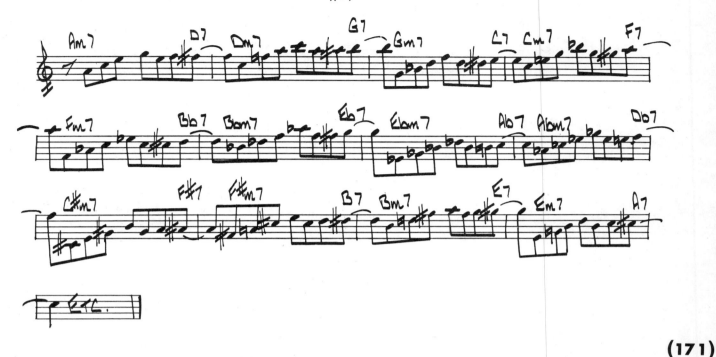

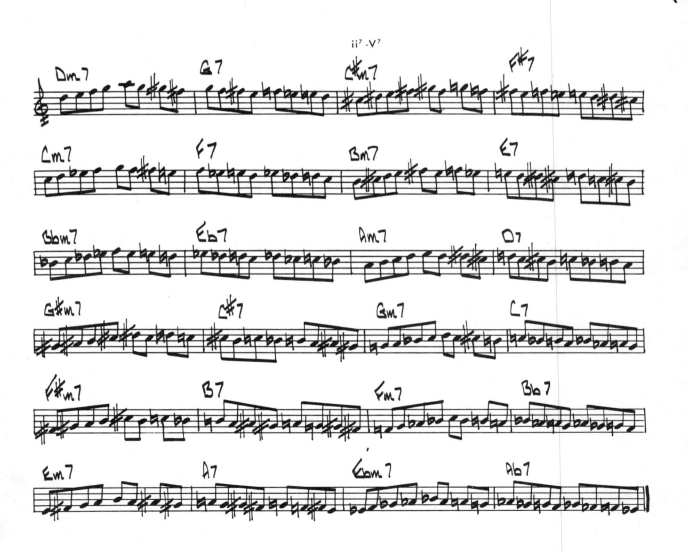

(173)

(174)

$I^6\text{-}ii^7\text{-}\sharp iv^7 IV^7$

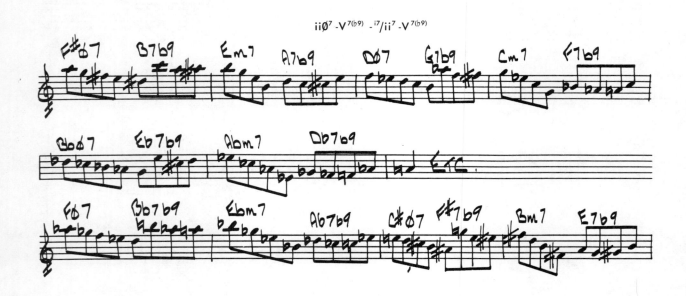

$ii\emptyset^7\text{-}V^{7(b9)}\text{-}i^7/ii^7\text{-}V^{7(b9)}$

$V^{7(b9)}/V - V^{7(b9)} - i^{6}$

(176)

(177)

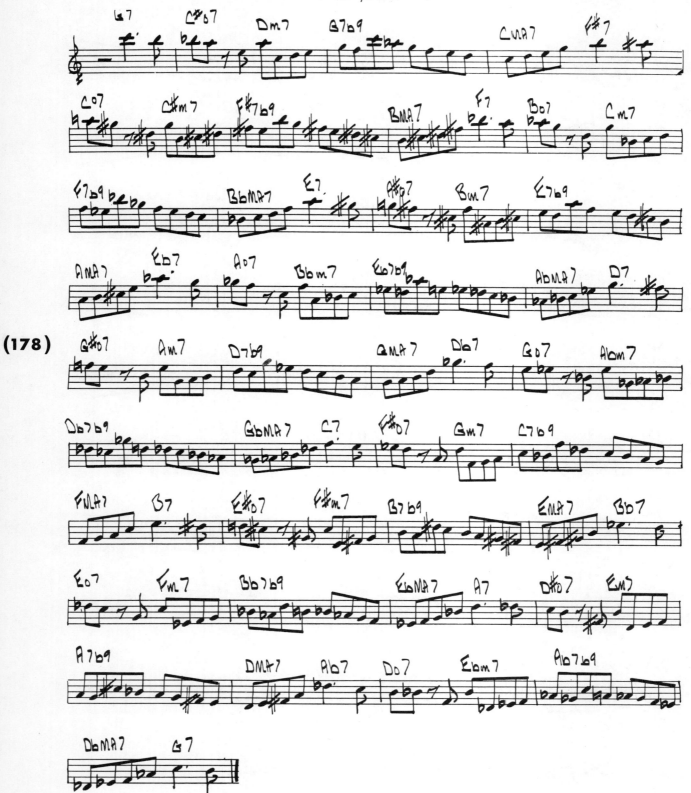

(178)

(179)

(180)

(181)

I(V⁷/ii)-ii⁷

(182)

Common jazz song forms

Chapter 10

(184)   **Simple Form**   Form in music—or for that matter, in any artistic discipline—refers to the organizational plan or layout of the work being considered. The question of form should be viewed from the point of view of organic organizational unfolding, not as a preconceived mold into which music is poured. The form of a piece is adjusted by the composer to fit the needs of the musical ideas. All too often a misconception exists that seems to dictate that the process works the other way around; that is, that musical concepts are crammed into a structured body of rigidity much as bricks and mortar would be applied to the structural framework of steel beams in a building. This is not to say, however, that one cannot codify and generalize regarding form; for, with all of the vagaries present in a given musical situation it is true that certain basic forms exist that aid the musician in organizing his or her materials.

In terms of jazz improvisation the form takes on a slightly different meaning than it does in classical music. In jazz the form of the piece, which includes the harmonic, melodic, and rhythmic elements as aspects integral to the structure, becomes the model upon which the improvisor refers in his solos. The form then in jazz is more of a reference point than it is in classical music. The jazz musician must have a comprehension of the form of the work being performed in order to improvise effectively. The better he understands the melodic structure, the harmonic plan, and the rhythmic life of the piece the better his improvisation will be. This is a fact not well understood by many not familiar with the rigors of jazz improvisation. All too often one finds an attitude prevalent amongst the unknowing indicative of a belief that the jazz musician literally "makes up" anything he pleases on the spot. This attitude obviously does not take into account the discipline the "form" imposes upon the jazz performer. And the more complete the knowledge of the form is, the better the improvisation is likely to be.

As in classical music, the melodic structure and the harmonic plan dictate the essence of the form. Motific congruence and a logical harmonic plan give life to the music. And, as in classical music, the motifs may be short, long, syncopated, and/or grouped into phrases. The harmonic rhythm (the relative rate of harmonic change) may be rapid or slow, the root relationships may be cyclic (e.g., cycle of fifths) or involve a mixture of conjunct and disjunct root connections.

Interestingly, some of the more simple forms in jazz may be found in music of the 1960s and 1970s. Many pieces exist from this period that involve melodic materials evolving out of one to four chord changes for the entire life of the piece. Tunes such as "Impressions" by John Coltrane, "Maiden Voyage" by Herbie Hancock, and "So What" by Miles Davis are illustrative of this principle.

In these works the melodic ideas are conceived around a basis of limited harmonic rhythm. Curiously, this type of form puts a great demand upon the improvisor to create effectively, for the player cannot rely upon patterns geared to chord changes that may give the impression of improvisational dexterity where none or little exists. Over a harmonic plateau that is relatively stable, the performer must be as inventive as he can possibly be in order to give a sense of balance and forward motion to his improvisation.

Most of the tunes of this type fall into structures of three basic types

A A   A B   A

In the composition below entitled "Tired of These Games" we see a basic A A structure, with each section encompassing eight measures. The second A is, in reality, a modified form of the first eight measures. Hence, we might more accurately wish to label this form as A A[1] to indicate the fact that the second section is melodically and harmonically altered from the first. However, the basic rhythmic design carries over to the second section, giving the appearance that the second half of the piece constitutes a modification of the first half. The harmonic rhythm of two chord changes per measure is found throughout the piece. Note that we have here two chord pairs: $D^{7(\sharp9)}$ and $G^{7(9)}$ in the first section, with $G\sharp m^9$ and EMA^7 in the second section, indicating the kind of harmonic stabilization alluded to earlier. The $D^{7(\sharp9)}$, $G^{7(9)}$ set is a more functionally related pair, because the root motion from D to G is a common fifth (or fourth) relationship. The $G\sharp m^9$ and EMA^7 set is not as common in terms of functional harmonic direction, inasmuch as the root relationship is one of a minor sixth (upward) or a major third (downward). However, the $G\sharp m^9$ and the EMA^7 chord are related significantly by virtue of common tone relationship:

$$
\begin{array}{lll}
A\sharp & & \\
F\sharp & & \\
D\sharp & \longleftrightarrow & D\sharp \\
B & \longleftrightarrow & B \\
G\sharp & \longleftrightarrow & G\sharp \\
& & E \\
G\sharp m^9 & & EMA^7
\end{array}
$$

(186)

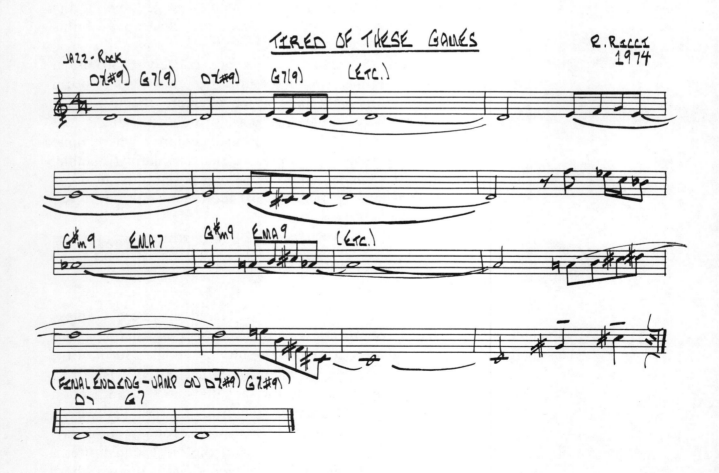

"Looking Ahead" is another example of a basic form alternating in segments we may characterize as A B. The B section here is eight measures in length, while A is six measures long. As in "Tired of These Games" we have two chord sets that alternate within each section:

A section: F^7 sus. $4/F^{13}$
B section: Gb^7 sus. $4/Bb^{13}$

When the chord pairs shift, the melodic line is changed and we move into the B section. Note that the chord pairs in this tune are more closely matched in that the changes for the B section are transposed up a half-step from those in the A section. The harmonic rhythm is very periodic throughout, with each chord change taking one measure. One can easily see how a tune such as this lends itself to the kind of melodic "stretching out" on the part of the improvisor, since one has essentially to deal with only two basic chords, F^{13} and Gb^{13}. The suspended quality of the chords which precede F^{13} and G^{13} involve a slight change in inflection as they move to the straight dominant-quality chord. In other words, the suspended fourth element here may be viewed as a modification of the basic dominant chord that follows, not as a chord that implies substantial new direction in improvisation. The suspended fourth chord is, in reality, a dominant seventh chord with an impeded element (the perfect fourth) replacing (usually temporarily) the third of the dominant seventh chord.

(187)

LOOKING AHEAD

R. RICCI
1975

We should mention another type of tune in this general category, although it is not as common as the two kinds previously discussed. This type of tune is more "through-composed"; that is, it does not employ sections or sectional contrast as do the other two types. The form of such a tune may be regarded as comprising just an A section; often it takes one melodic motif and works it out in the piece. Such is the case with "Charlie Horse," which appears below. The main motif is seen in the first two measures. It is then repeated and modified through the techniques of intervallic compression (measures 3 and 4), intervallic expansion (measures 5 and 6), intervallic compression and melodic extension (measures 9 through 12), and rhythmic/metric displacement (measures 13 through 19). Obviously, the entire piece is based rather exclusively on the motific elements presented in measures 1 and 2. Further, the chord changes are limited, with only six different chords heard throughout the piece. The harmonic rhythm tends to be static, with fairly long stretches occupied by a given chord. In this type of tune the players will often choose to ignore the chord changes of the piece, and focus instead on one central chordal element. Here, the players are instructed to base their improvisations on Cm^{11}, the central chord of the piece and the tonal center of "Charlie Horse."

(188)

In "Thinking," a little ballad in 12/8 meter, we see another example of an A form. Here the rather continuous eighth-note motion, the even interaction between the right and left hand, and the ebb and flow of the melodic curve keep a certain constancy on the surface as well as in the heart of the composition. Some might wish to see this piece as an A (measures 1 through 9), A' (measures 9 through 18) because the main motive heard first in measure 1 reappears in measure 9. Modification of the melodic direction becomes evident if measures 9 through 18 are compared with 1 through 9. However, whether one regards this divide as important in terms of the overall form or not, we can readily see that one idea rather continuously permeates the entire piece.

(189)

(190)

A B A
FORM
One of the most common forms for jazz pieces is the ABA form. In its most typical configuration one finds AABA, with each letter representing an eight-measure section, all the A parts being virtually identical. In reality then, an AABA structure constitutes a thirty-two-measure form of which there are really only two contrasting parts: A and B. The B section, typically called the "bridge" or "release," has the critical function of contrasting with the A part. This may be achieved in a variety of ways. Modulation to a related key area, rhythmic alteration, or melodic re-

structuring are perhaps the most common ways of achieving contrast in the B section. A debate is sometimes carried on as to just how different and how important the bridge should be in an AABA tune. Some claim that it must function as a not-too-interesting relief to the A section, and thereby never assume primacy over the A part. Others contend that the B part must be fully developed and solid in its own right. In reality many successful popular songs and jazz pieces may be cited that are illustrative of both positions.

Two bossa novas are found below, both illustrative of the AABA form. Let us take each one and examine the entire structure. "Nimo's Lilt" has the following plan:

A 11 measures (including first ending)
A 11 measures (including second ending)
B 8 measures
A 8 measures
Coda 11 measures
Total 49 measures

Some observations as to the length of the sections are in order. The A section here is atypical in that it is eleven measures in length instead of the more commonly found eight-measure section. This fact, however, need not trouble us, for many songs and jazz tunes of the current period have departed from the strict thirty-two-measure format. The coda is, from a musical point of view, merely an elaboration and extension of the melodic and harmonic material found in A. The tonality of the piece, A♭ major, is not immediately clear at the outset of the tune. It is confirmed in the first and second endings as well as in the last seven bars of the coda, which fluctuate back and forth between A♭MA⁷ and EMA⁷. The B section is melodically varied from A, yet incorporates some of the rhythmic and motific elements of A into its structure (for example, the rhythmic pattern ♪♪♪). One can argue again as to the precise nature of the contrast afforded by B, but perhaps the best way to look at it is that B must be on the one hand congruent with A while different on the other.

"Betty's Bossa" has this plan:

Introduction 3 measures
A 8 measures (including first ending)
A 8 measures (including second ending)
B 8 measures
A 6 measures
Coda 8 measures

(193)

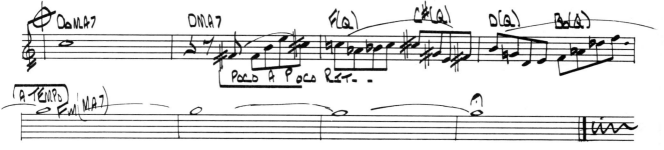

In "Betty's Bossa" the B section has more of a truly contrasting nature than in "Nimo's Lilt." It, too, however, contains a coda. In this case the material for the coda is drawn from the opening measures of the introduction, thus giving a "rounded" feeling of form to the piece.

A more "straight-ahead" jazz tune is "Young Spraggins."
The formal plan here is as follows:

A 15 measures (including first ending)
A 15 measures (including second ending)
B 8 measures
A 15 measures
Coda 12 measures

(194)

Some features of this tune are worth commenting upon. Note that the A section contains one measure in a 2/4 meter. This again is an element more likely to be found in newer tunes. In fact, many jazz pieces have been written that make metric changes a focal point of the formal design. "Young Spraggins" also uses quartal harmony rather extensively. Since the harmonic rhythm of this piece is so quick it is suggested that for the purpose of improvisation the following sequence of chords be followed:

$$\|:B\flat MA^7|B\flat MA^7|D\flat MA^7|D\flat MA^7|B\flat MA^7|B\flat MA^7|D\flat MA^7|D\flat MA^7|$$
$$|A\flat MA^7|A\flat MA^7|BMA^7|BMA^7|B\flat MA^7|B\flat MA^7|A\flat MA^7|A\flat MA^7:\|$$

This sixteen-measure sequence draws its form from the major seventh chordal layout found in the opening four measures of the piece. As with the bossa nova tunes, the coda here employs structural fragments of the A section.

THE BLUES In the annals of American music, the tremendous importance and influence of the blues can hardly be overestimated. Its spirit and flavor pervade almost all jazz, and its effect has been felt in country, pop, and rock music. For some, the blues connotes melancholy; the lament of great artists like Bessie Smith or Ma Rainey complaining about a man who has strayed or been lost for good. Others associate the blues with Black work spirituals or gospel chants. LeRoi Jones claims that the blues originated directly out of the field shout in the old South—a cry that served as a personal communication between the slaves in the field and one man's personal reaction to work and life around him. Whatever its origin, the blues at its inception was an emotional outcry that depended upon a fresh and untamed nature for its very emotional substance.

The "formal" blues, twelve bars in length (sometimes eight or sixteen bars), was a later evolutionary product of the coarse, rough, and uninhibited blues of the field.

It is outside the scope of this book to deal at length with the history of the blues. Many excellent works are available that document the development of this style and form (it is both!).

Most blues tunes follow a repetitive or cyclic twelve-measure form. The twelve-measure sequence repeats for as long as is appropriate to the piece in question. Three basic chords based on I (tonic), IV (subdominant), and V (dominant) serve as the harmonic nucleus for a typical blues within the twelve-bar framework.

I I I I IV IV I I V IV I I

If we pick a specific key such as G Major, we can illustrate the fact that the basic chord type upon which the blues relies is the dominant seventh chord.

G⁷ G⁷ G⁷ G⁷ C⁷ C⁷ G⁷ G⁷ D⁷ C⁷ G⁷ G⁷

Crucial to melodic inflection above these chords is the use of so-called "blue" notes in the lead part above the harmonic foundation. In Example 1, the two most common "blue" notes in the key of G would be the lowered third (B flat) and the lowered seventh (F natural):

EXAMPLE 1

These two blue notes do not necessarily supplant the use of the ordinary notes of the major scale. They may be used in conjunction with the "regular" degrees of the scale in melodic movement. Example 2 illustrates a possible melodic configuration over the harmonic foundation of G⁷ employing both regular and blue notes (marked with *).

(196)

EXAMPLE 2

When the chord changes to C⁷, the blue notes change from B flat and F natural to E flat and B flat, the lowered third and seventh of the C major scale. Notice that the lowered seventh of C (B flat) and the lowered third of G (B flat) are the same note. This "common" tone makes it likely that the improvisor will carry the use of B flat over into bars 5 and 6 of the blues progression:

EXAMPLE 3

The use of common tones built on blue notes of the three chords of the blues leads to the use of a device called a "riff." A riff is usually a short melodic/rhythmic cell that is played repetitively above the chord changes. The riff below is a five-note group first heard in measure 1. In Example 4, notice how it can be utilized almost continuously over the twelve-bar sequence of blues changes, creating a form in the process.

EXAMPLE 4

(197)

The riff in this case is set off not only by its configuration around the blue note B flat but also by its rhythmic design. Such a conjunction of melodic and rhythmic interplay leads to the design of a successful riff. The riff in the example above undergoes various alterations, most of them quite simple, as it progresses through the twelve-bar sequence. The alterations are usually intervallic, as in measure 2, where the F natural replaces the original E on the third beat, or rhythmic as in measure 3, where the third beat moves ahead into two more eighth notes in a downward curve. However, it is important to notice that in measure 5 the riff returns in its original form. The movement to the IV chord here often necessitates the return of the riff in its original as a codifying factor in the blues. Most rock and jazz blues take a "head" or theme built out of a riff figure and utilize it as the primary theme of the blues, heard in the first and last choruses as an identifying structure. In jazz especially, the middle choruses, which may be any number in length, are set aside for improvisation on the melodic basis of the riff and its supporting chord changes. One way of evaluating a jazz or rock artist is to listen carefully to these interior metamorphoses of the blues head, noting how successfully (or unsuccessfully) the artist is able to breathe creative life into the melodic and harmonic cells of the twelve-bar sequence.

A word is also in order here regarding the rhythmic design of blue riffs. The examples above have been indicated in simple, standard notation. However, this notation is not precisely correct for the proper "feel" of the blues. It is virtually impossible to indicate with our present system of notation the exact rhythm of such melodies. For example, the blues riff above is rhythmically somewhere between:

EXAMPLE 5

In reality this presents little problem for the person wanting to transcribe the feeling of such melodies. There is a certain rhythmic bending or anticipation of the notes in rock and jazz (particularly in jazz) that gives the tune its identification as a jazz or rock piece. Without this rhythmic feeling one immediately senses that there is something "wrong" with the rendition. This often happens, for example, when a person who is used to playing classical music attempts for the first time to play jazz or rock.

Example 6 is more in the rock than jazz style, but it nonetheless illustrates the use of the flat third, the flat seventh, and the rhythmic design of a melody in rock.

EXAMPLE 6

Jazz artists often include more complex chords of the ninth, eleventh, and thirteenth in their blues changes, as well as adding subsidiary chordal movement around the basic pillars of I, IV, and V. Example 7 shows a set of blues changes in the key of F Major as a progressive jazz artist might render it:

EXAMPLE 7

(199)

Notice in this case how the chords are more complex, and how more chord changes are found. For example, the second bar contains a movement to the B♭⁷ chord; bar 8 contains a secondary dominant relationship to the Gm⁷ chord of bar 9, which in itself is a chord not found in the more basic blues pattern; a turnaround is found in bars 11 and 12, based on a III–VI–II–V root pattern. This has the function of guiding the ear back to the start of the blues and the I chord.

Many blues heads involve motific repetition as the basis of their formal design. In "Rolf, Rolf" a repetitious rhythmic figure is heard throughout the entire twelve-bar blues as the chords change below. The chordal pattern is the basic format discussed earlier.

Rolf, Rolf

R. Ricci
1975

(200)

In "Wheaton Blues" we see some changes from the standard chord progressions delineated above. Although the main outline of the chords stay the same (e.g., F^7 in measures 4 and 17; C^7 in measures 7 and 19; G^7 in measures 10 and 22), there are some additional passing-chord changes that are perfectly possible within the context of the main blues framework. This piece is a twice-repeated twelve-bar blues, and some comparisons between the two sections in terms of the chords utilized reveal some of the differences in harmonic syntax. Compare, for example, measures 2 and 14. Measure 2 employs three linear passing chords moving upwards in chromatic half-steps, whereas measure 14 employs a standard IV (F^7) chord. Note that measures 11 and 12 employ a typical turnaround of C^7–A^7–D^7–G^7 before the second twelve-bar blues begins. It should be stressed that in terms of the overall twelve-bar blues structure there are certain harmonic pillars that rarely vary. Those are the I chord in the first measure, the IV chord in the fifth measure, the I chord in the seventh measure, and the I chord in the eleventh measure. Outside and around these harmonic motions all sorts of passing and cyclic motions may occur, as long as the main structural framework of the blues stays intact.

WHEATON BLUES

R. Ricci
1976

(201)

Another even more highly irregular blues tune is "Weird Blues." This "doubled" blues of twenty-four measures employs the chromatic harmonic relationship to an even greater degree than "The Brat." Note that the following chromatic pairs appear throughout the piece:

Measures 1–8 :	$F^{7(\sharp 11)}$–$F\sharp^{7(\sharp 11)}$
Measures 9–12:	$Am^{7(9)}$–$B\flat m^{7(9)}$
Measures 13–16:	$F^{7(\sharp 11)}$–$F\sharp^{7(\sharp 11)}$
Measures 17–18:	$E\flat^{7(\sharp 9)}$–$E^{7(\sharp 9)}$
Measures 19–20:	$D\flat^{7(\sharp 9)}$–$D^{7(\sharp 9)}$
Measures 21–24:	$F^{7(\sharp 11)}$–$F\sharp^{7(\sharp 11)}$

The tonal framework is clearly F^7, as it would be in any typical F blues. The return to F^7 in measures 13 to 16 and 21 to 24 clearly frames and relates the piece of a typical blues structure. Perhaps the most unusual feature here is the absence of IV ($B\flat^7$). Instead, measures 9 to 12 employ Am^7 in the "secondary tonal area." Nonetheless, the tune is a blues, albeit a rather irregular blues form.

In the tune "The Brat" we see a good example of a twelve-bar structure which, in a loose sense, is a blues tune. Note that the first three measures contain the C^7–F^7–C^7 motion so typical to the blues. Past that point, into measures 4 through 8 the harmonic progression is essentially chromatic and passing. Measures 9 through 12 reinforce the blues feeling with the harmonic retrogression of Bb⁷–Ab⁷ occurring twice. Then, the G⁷ (♯11) chord in the latter part of measure 12 prepares the C⁷ chord returning to measure 1. So, this type of tune is a good example of an irregular blues that utilizes certain harmonic features common to standard blues.

Several of these compositions were made possible through a grant of the Faculty Research Fund at Western Michigan University.

The development of a jazz solo for the beginning improvisor

Chapter 11

(206)

The organization and development of a good jazz solo presents certain problems which the performer must learn to deal with on an individual basis. The idea that the truly great jazz musician is someone who either has magical and mystical powers or must sell a portion of his soul each time he produces a brilliant solo is far from reality. The fact is, this ability comes from thousands of hours of very methodical and disciplined practice in which jazz scales and patterns like those presented in this text, and countless others, are memorized backward and forward, inside and out. These are then put to the test through trial and error in playing sessions night after night, year after year, until they begin to take shape. True, those who are born with a good ear and the ability to concentrate and memorize in this intense fashion will have an easier time in developing improvisational skills, and indeed there are those who are truly gifted in this area, but it still remains that the most important factor is a great sense of determination, dedication, and discipline—without which, inherent abilities notwithstanding, there is no hope.

There is another obstacle that you as a student must recognize. Throughout your development as a musician, you have gained skill in the reading and interpretation of music. You may also have developed an admirable technique, but you must approach improvisation as if you and your instrument had never met. In a real musical sense, you must learn to crawl before walking and learn to walk before running. Unfortunately, most students do not have the determination to cope with this situation and see it through.

Along these lines it will be difficult in the following material to simply play whole notes and half-notes when your fingers are capable of moving much faster. It may also be hard to understand how suggested exercises will develop the sense of rhythm, note, and chord relationships required in the performance of a quality solo.

When you first approach a tune utilizing an involved set of chord changes, write out the roots of the chords with note values corresponding to the duration of each chord. Example 1 is a jazz blues with whole notes and half-notes filled in for the respective duration of the chords.*

EXAMPLE 1

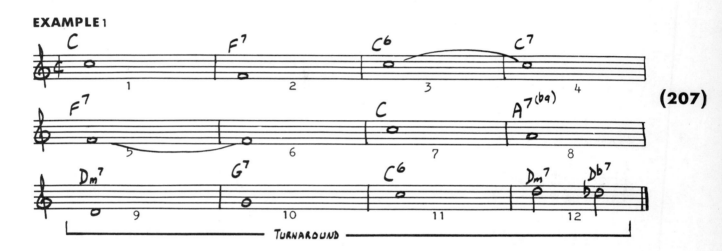

(207)

On the first four or five performances of this solo limit your-self to playing the notes written as illustrated in Example 1. Listen carefully for the quality of each chord and the relative duration of the chords. Also note the sound of the movement of one chord to another, especially in the turnaround.

On the next four or five performances of the solo continue to play only the roots of the chords but take time to *write out* some rhythmic variations as demonstrated in Example 2. Make a special effort to accent the downbeats of each measure, especially those in which the chord changes. After a number of repetitions of the written rhythms, improvise your own while continuing to consciously accent the downbeats and chord changes.

---

* The authors highly recommend the use of the multi-volume set of im-provisation records by Jamey Aebersold. They provide rhythm section tracks over which the student may practice improvising. Volume II, *Nothin' But the Blues,* is especially appropriate for use here. Jamey Aebersold, 1211-D Aeber-sold Drive, New Albany, Indiana 47150.

EXAMPLE 2

Again listen to the sound of each chord and, especially in this early encounter with simple rhythmic development, to the relative duration of the chords as related to one another.

The next step in the development of this solo involves the outlining of each chord. Take time to write out basic triads and seventh chords using simple rhythms, accenting downbeats and chord changes as illustrated in Example 3.

(208)

EXAMPLE 3

After four or five times through the chorus, experiment by varying the rhythms played in each measure along with the chord structure, always being aware of the passage of rhythmic time and the necessity to change chords at the correct moment with good rhythmic flow and continuity (Example 4).

EXAMPLE 4

While continuing to listen as before to chord quality, relative duration, and sound movement, note the common tones that exist from one chord to the next. For example, the root of the I⁷ chord in measure 4 sustains as the fifth of the IV⁷ chord in measure 5.

The next step in continuing to develop this solo should involve an attempt to discover ascending and descending scale progressions through the chord changes. As in Examples 5(a), 5(b), 5(c), 6(a), 6(b), and 6(c), start on one of the notes in the first chord of the solo and try to develop scales through the following chord changes by selecting notes that fit in each chord, using passing tones (PT) where necessary. Follow this by finding sequential patterns, scale or otherwise, that also fit the chord pattern (Example 7). Once these scale and sequential patterns are discovered you should play them numerous times, listening to how the notes succeed in linking the chord changes together. Add rhythms to the scales to add interest and variety.

(209)

EXAMPLE 5

EXAMPLE 6

(210)

EXAMPLE 7

In the next step, relate each chord in the solo to its appropriate scale as determined by its function. Use the material and charts in Chapter III to complete this task. Write each scale down in proper sequence with the corresponding chord above, as demonstrated in Example 8. Begin the next playing session by running each scale in the allotted time allowed by the rhythmic duration of each chord. Follow this by inverting alternate scales so that a more melodic and connected motion is achieved (Example 9). This might necessitate using only portions of some scales and extending others. You should play each of these variations many times until they feel comfortable, taking care to listen for new relationships between chords, notes within chords, and rhythmic tendencies. Keep in mind that trial and error is the best means to success. This is different from the technique employed in performing classical music. In jazz you must not be afraid to make errors when you strike out in the direction of improvisation. Use your ear and musical intellect, learn from errors, and you will eventually develop the confidence imperative for the jazz performer.

(211)

EXAMPLE 8

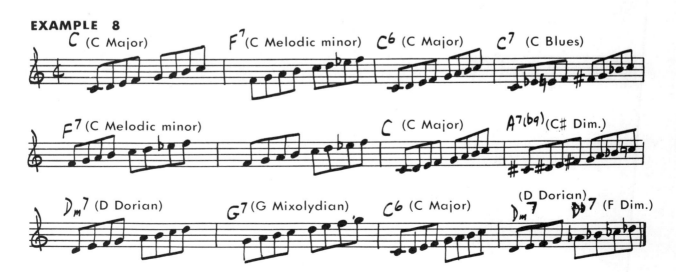

EXAMPLE 9

The final step in the development of this solo involves the combination of jazz scales with chords to create more interest and variation. This in turn could be enhanced by the addition of chromatic embellishment, the insertion of jazz patterns—especially in ii⁷–V⁷–I progressions—and the use of chord substitutions. As before, give special attention to rhythmic development.

Example 10 shows a simple chorus written over the blues changes. Note that the first eight measures of the solo are mostly chord-oriented and that the last four measures are more scale- and pattern-oriented. Chromatic embellishment is used in measures 3, 5, 6, 10, 11, and 12, and in every case, this embellishment works hand in hand with sequential movement.

EXAMPLE 10

Example 11 shows a chorus derived almost entirely from a sequential pattern. The notes in this pattern are sometimes altered to fit the chord sequence and scales. Chromatic embellishment is also used in measures 2, 6, 9, 10, and 11. Note that the use of sequence often leads to a rather stagnant rhythm—in this case, the running eighth note.

EXAMPLE 11

Example 12 demonstrates a much more involved use of sequence and pattern. The flatted fifth and ninth have arbitrarily been added in measures 1 and 2 and the true pattern of the sequence has been kept, despite the fact that it leads to incorrect notes in relation to the chord changes (measures 3 and 4). The reasoning behind this is that the tension thus created is released as the pattern reaches the IV⁷ chord in the fifth measure, resulting in a very interesting effect. The same idea occurs in measures 8 and 9. The *direction and drive* created by the pattern is deemed more important than the fact that the F♯ major scale is being used over a Dm⁷ chord. Again note the static (eighth-note) rhythm inherent in this type of solo. It would be assumed that preceding and subsequent choruses would develop this aspect to a greater degree, thus giving the total solo a nice feeling of contrast. Again, chromatic embellishment is found throughout.

(213)

EXAMPLE 12

In developing a solo on a tune that utilizes only one chord (as in many contemporary jazz/rock works) or a small number of chord changes, each played for a considerable length of time (as in many modal-oriented works), a different set of problems confronts the player. Although dealing with many chords and the inherent problem of learning to play through the changes, as previously discussed, is not of concern, the player must readily recognize the need for more rhythmic interest and a variety of melodic content to offset the lack of these in the chord progression.

The following steps might help you to organize your thoughts and develop a more meaningful solo when confronted with this situation.

1. Select the best scale to fit the chord change. If there is any question as to the scale, determine what scale is used in the melodic material and use it as the primary scale in the improvisation.
2. Work out a number of three-, four-, and five-note melodic motifs that can be stated in the beginning and used for development as the solo progresses.
3. Develop an equal number of rhythmic motifs in relation to the melodic motifs that can also be used in the same fashion.
4. Write out an extended series of patterns based on the scale. Begin with patterns based solely on the scale and progress to those involving more chromatic embellishment.
5. Conceive the solo so that it develops rhythmically, melodically, and in intensity to a climax that can be resolved in the solo's conclusion.

Regarding the materials and concepts presented in this chapter, it must be noted that there are many factors not discussed that will have a great effect on how they are put to use. For instance, the style of the tune in question: for our demonstrations we selected a jazz blues. The situation discussed and the presentation of materials would be entirely different if we were to apply the concepts to a rock blues, modal blues, or even a gospel blues. Each different style requires a different approach, even when the chords and scales utilized remain the same. The blues illustrated was a medium- to up-tempo example. If the tempo is changed, new criteria must be considered. If the chord changes were altered either to simplify or to complicate the harmonic flow, different approaches would be necessary.

All this leads to a most important point: everything you do in the field of improvisation must be balanced by a large portion of listening. We have made no attempt in the course of this text to dictate or even discuss style or related areas like phrasing and articulation. The materials and ideas presented here will prove valuable only to the extent that they are applied to vast and varied listening and performance experiences.

Solo
transcription

Chapter 12

In continuing to stress the importance of listening and imitating, **(217)** we must emphasize the need for the close study of recorded solos. The transcription of recorded solos is a most important item in the development of improvisational skills. It requires close attention, repetitive listening, recognition of phrasing and rhythmic nuance in a melodic situation, training fingers to respond and recreate things heard, and much, much more.

There is no real secret to the process of transcription and probably little consolation in the fact that the more you do, the easier it will become. The following suggestions should help.

1. Equipment is most important! A good turntable with 45, 33 1/3, and 16 rpm settings along with variable pitch control is desirable. Access to a reel-to-reel tape recorder is also helpful.

2. Listen to the solo in question repeatedly until you have the melodic pattern memorized to the extent that you can scat along in unison with the solo.

3. If it is a standard tune or blues, try to obtain a copy of the head and chord changes. Revert to this material when in doubt about the tonal centers of the piece and for help in finding the possible chord and scale patterns a soloist might be using.

4. In order to save wear on the record, tape the solo at 7 1/2 ips (inches per second) and play it back a phrase at a time. Use your ear, your instrument, a piano, or anything else available

to help you find the correct notes. If a passage is very fast or for some other reason needs clarification, slow the tape recorder to 3 3/4 ips. This will cut the speed in half and also put the passage down an octave. To further reduce the speed, set the turntable at 16 rpm (for a 33 1/3 rpm record) and record it at 7 1/2 ips. If you play this back at 3 3/4 ips, the speed will be four times as slow as the original and two octaves lower.

5. Always write down the solo being transcribed. First, draw only the note heads. Second, draw in the bar lines, and finally, notate the correct rhythms.

6. Edit all notes for correct accidentals and check again for correct notation of rhythms.

7. Play the transcription with the record (or tape) at half-speed and again check for errors.

8. Play the solo with the record at normal speed. Make every effort to imitate all articulations and phrasings exactly as performed by the original artist.

9. Note any melodic sequence, pattern, or progression you especially like. Write it in all twelve keys as demonstrated in earlier chapters and commit it to memory for future use in other situations.

Make it a practice to transcribe solos from all competent performers, no matter what instrument they may play. The more you widen your scope and perspective, the more opportunity you have to develop your own abilities and style.

For transcribed solos that have been made available through publication, check the following sources:
Issues often contain transcribed and annotated solos.
Down Beat Magazine
222 W. Adams Street
Chicago, Ill. 60606
A series of books, each containing hundreds of transcribed solos.
Jazz Style and Analysis
Down Beat Workshop Publications
222 W. Adams Street
Chicago, Ill. 60606
Over 200 solos have been transcribed and are available
John Coltrane Solos and Eric Dolphy Solos
c/o Mr. Andrew White
Musical Enterprises, Inc.,
4830 South Dakota Avenue, N.E.
Washington, D.C. 20017

(218)